Jet with Kids

Taking the Fear Out of Flying...
WITH YOUR KIDS!

By Anya Clowers, RN, Traveling Mom

Jet With Kids- Taking the Fear Out of Flying...WITH YOUR KIDS! is the ultimate resource for anyone flying with children. Experts including flight attendants, a reservation agent, gate agents, a pediatrician, travel agents, a pilot, and multiple traveling moms provide incredible tips, product suggestions and product reviews, as well as numerous links to informative sites. Written by a traveling mom, who was comfortable with the flight process until she had to face a flight with a baby – her own!

Jet With Kids:
Taking the Fear Out of Flying
WITH YOUR KIDS!

2

1st Edition Copyright © 2006 Jet Seven, Inc. All rights reserved.

Published by Jet Seven, Inc. Gold River, CA 95670

Production coordinated by Rachel Snyder

ISBN 978-0-6151-3757-5

Library of Congress Control Number: 2007922435

Printed in the United States of America

Cover design by Ovi Dogar
Photographs provided by author

WHAT OTHERS ARE SAYING ABOUT
JET WITH KIDS

"Jet with Kids is a wonderful resource for families who travel. Anya Clowers has included everything a parent needs to know about flying with their children. I wish I had had this resource when my kids were small, because I would have been more prepared for flying with children and would have avoided many of the problems I encountered. The many website links included in Jet with Kids make preparing for a flight and gathering the necessary tools and information very easy. I highly recommend reading Jet with Kids before you take your next flight!"
- *Sara Galbraith, M.S., MFT (Family Therapist) Traveling Mom of 2 Children – ages 15 and 12; Davis, CA*

"Jet With Kids is not just a list of what to pack. Nor is it a 'Best Of' of parent advice. It is rather a combination of personal experience, aggregated data, professional input, practical advice and frank honesty. It is written one parent to another and difficult to put down once it's picked up! Such a resource was unavailable for parents when I was traveling with my then-toddler, and as a result I developed my own product around this very subject. I am so impressed with Ms. Clowers's professionalism and pragmatism that I recommend and link to JetWithKidsClub.com from nearly every page of my website, www.goodlittletraveler.com."
- *Scotty Kober, Creator, the I'm A Good Little Traveler! Shae by Air DVD Toolkit*

"I've vacationed with my kids from Maine to California and I thought I knew how to travel with kids. Then I read Jet With Kids and I wondered how my children survived. The practical suggestions, expert opinions (not your uncle Wilbur) and especially the myths that this book dispels makes it a must read. I never knew that ear pain while flying could be avoided until now. This book is a fabulous resource to anyone who has kids, is thinking of having kids, or has seen kids...it's really that good."
- *Ron Cloer, Traveling Dad of 3 Children – ages 12, 8, and 3; Indianapolis, Indiana*

"A must read to ensure an enjoyable flight with your children. Excellent organized information!"
- *Janet, Grandmother of 6 year old, Teacher, Frequent Flier; Fair Oaks, CA*

"I thought all of the information was laid out well for parents to understand. The real-life stories enhanced the chapters so readers could relate with the author. An excellent book to recommend to parents if they are traveling anywhere!"
- *Jenny Olson, Mom of 1 year old, Teacher; Holmen, WI*

Jet With Kids:
Taking the Fear Out of Flying
WITH YOUR KIDS!

4

"I cannot think of a thing that you left out. The section about what to pack for the plane was extremely helpful as that is an area that I tend to overdue. Overall, in my opinion, this is the 'go to' book for parents, grandparents, friends, etc. who find themselves flying with little ones. There is a wealth of information regarding the ins and outs of an airport, making your way through security with your sanity still in check to the dreaded lost luggage. Web sites to all of the great products listed in the book was a real time saver for over committed Mom's, like myself. The best piece of advice that I have learned is that our children pick up on our attitudes and stress levels, so keep your cool and enjoy yourselves!
You have a winner here, Anya. It really is a wonderful resource for anyone that travels."
- Tracy McCormick, Traveling Mom of 2 Children – ages 7 and 2; Lincoln, CA

"Jet With Kids: Taking the Fear Out of Flying With Your Kids" is a book whose time has come. This is a great source of information to help parents navigate and make informed decisions about all aspects of flying with children. Anya Clowers has obviously devoted a tremendous amount of time into researching and providing the first essential resource for parents that will educate them on the planning, preparation and safety aspects of traveling with a young child by air; as well as how to make the journey as comfortable and enjoyable as possible. All parents who fly with children, especially those who are embarking on their 'maiden voyages', will gain valuable information from this book that will absolutely make the trip easier and more enjoyable for the whole family."
- Lorna Evenden, Co-founder TravelingWithKids.com

"I really appreciated the information about products that help you transport the car seat through the airport and onto the plane. I wish I had known about these products before lugging a car seat through several different airports! Jet With Kids is a valuable resource for anyone traveling with children, full of helpful websites and up to the minute safety information."
- Diane, Pregnant with 2nd Child and Mom of 2 year old; Rochester, MN

**We welcome your feedback and testimonials. Send an email to
info@JetWithKids.com

ALSO BY

Anya Clowers, RN, Traveling Mom

<u>So Your Child Is Flying Alone...What You Need to Know About Flying as an Unaccompanied Minor!</u>

Sign up for our
Jet With Kids Newsletter

at www.JetWithKidsClub.com

An informative, easy-to-read newsletter sent out via email 2-3 times per month.

Offering updated tips and recommendations, products and product reviews, as well as hyperlinks to new and useful websites, and much more!

Jet With Kids:
Taking the Fear Out of Flying
WITH YOUR KIDS!

6

Attention Airline Organizations, Travel Agents, and other travel suppliers:
Please contact us about quantity discounts for this book as well as a discount package containing this book (to prepare parents) and a DVD toolkit (to prepare children) for flying.

For more information, contact Rachel Snyder at 916-853-9619 or info@JetWithKidsClub.com.

Looking for a group fundraiser?
Contact us at info@JetWithKidsClub.com for more information.

Dedicated to California 6 ½

I love you guys –
and thank you for your support,
encouragement and love.

Table of Contents

Jet With Kids:
Taking the Fear Out of Flying
WITH YOUR KIDS!

10

HOW TO READ THIS RESOURCE

As a parent myself, I know that you are busy. I have set this resource up to save you time in many ways. If you only have short amounts of time in one sitting and want to read about certain topics, you can easily select that topic from the Table of Contents and read through that section. If you want a general overview of the whole flight process and are going to skim through the whole resource, important points are highlighted in boxes or underlined. And if you are wanting to get all the info., it is easy to read from start to finish.

Since I found a lot of great products and information online, I save you time and energy by including these links. Of course, the Internet is constantly changing, and if you encounter a broken link, please email us at support@JetWithKids.com so that we can fix the problem immediately.

One frustration that I encountered over and over again when I was trying to prepare for my first flights with my infant son, was that as I read someone's tips or talked to a mother about their favorite travel product, they would not remember where they got it or wouldn't mention it. Hours and hours of time were spent researching what to pack and what other parents' reviews were on products.

That is why in this resource, I have links to many of the products that I have found to be beneficial in travel. I was looking for products designed for children and travel – specifically airline travel. I have included many audio descriptions of these products for the traveling child (This is available in the audio version only-coming soon. For more information, send an email to info@JetWithKids.com)

I also added reviews about the products if I felt strongly about them or have used them frequently. I have not used all of these products and caution you that I do not take responsibility for any of them. I merely wanted to make it more convenient for you to fly

Jet With Kids:
Taking the Fear Out of Flying
WITH YOUR KIDS!

12

prepared (and save you time and energy searching for products). Some of my reviews are longer than most, but I included things that I would have liked to have known myself!

> **I also cannot stress enough that you know your children best and what will work with them. Please apply all suggestions only if age and developmentally appropriate. This resource is about what has worked for my family and for the people I have interviewed.**
>
> **By purchasing this you are acknowledging that you will take full responsibility for any actions resulting from the tips given in this resource. Consult your family physician before administering any supplements, vitamins, or medication to your child.**
>
> **The travel products are only suggestions and are ones that I prefer to use. They may not be appropriate in all situations. Please use your best judgment, as you will take responsibility for your decisions.**

I have also set up another website to make shopping on eBay easier for the traveling family; http://www.fundsfortravel.com is set up with the main page displaying travel products that are currently for sale on eBay. If you do not see the item that you are searching for, just search for that product in the search box located toward the top right of the page. You can also search by categories, which are located in the left column.

A fun feature of this site is the eBay Misspelling Tool - check it out! Try searching terms like luggage – often misspelled!

If you would like to recommend a product that you love or submit a review/testimonial, you can send me an email at info@JetWithKids.com. I am always updating this resource and welcome your ideas!

> **Please e-mail me at support@JetWithKids.com to report any problems with links not working correctly.**

The Resource Page

The Resource Page for this book is located at:
www.JetWithKidsClub.com/resources.html

The Products Page

Products mentioned in this book are listed in a convenient organized manner at:
www.JetWithKidsClub.com/products.html

Jet With Kids:
Taking the Fear Out of Flying
WITH YOUR KIDS!

14

ACKNOWLEDGEMENTS

Thank you so very much to those in the airline industry who have such an incredible passion for travel. I appreciate your time and energy, especially when some of you were facing very uncertain futures due to budget cuts.

The following is a list of 21 Travel Experts whose combined travel experience exceeds 450 years and makes this resource incredibly rare.

Role	Name/Title in Resource	Years of experience
Flight Attendant	**Flight Attendant A**	28
Flight Attendant	**Renée**	36
Flight Attendant	**Jan Brown-Lohr**	25
Flight Attendant	**Flight Attendant Karen**	29
Reservations Agent	**Reservations Agent**	7
Unaccompanied Minor	**Supervisor A**	8
Unaccompanied Minor	**Supervisor B**	14
Unaccompanied Minor	**Supervisor C**	8
Gate Agent	**Gate Agent Victoria**	23
Gate Agent	**Gate Agent A**	30
Gate Agent	**Gate Agent B**	28
Mom/Commercial Pilot	**Traveling Mom Carole**	13
Mom	**Traveling Mom Gilly**	6
Pediatrician	**Peter Contini, M.D.**	8
Travel Agent	**Kathryn Sudeikis, CTC**	35
Travel Agent/Airline Employee	**Bob Robar**	42
Single Parent Traveler	**Brenda Elwell**	40
Mom/Pilot/Website owner	**Beth McGregor**	4
Pilot	**Capt. Denny Fitch, Sr.**	41
Security	**Aviation Agent**	8
Grandma/Inventor	**Louise Stoll**	20
	Travel Experience	**453 years**

Thank you to Retired Flight Attendants Renée and Jan Brown-Lohr, as well as those flight attendants that remain anonymous sources of information for this resource. You all are a wonderful asset to the community of travelers – decades of service with a smile, and always focused on safety! Jan, you have been a source of motivation and encouragement. I am sorry that you experienced such a horrific event as the devastating crash, but am thankful that you chose to speak out in the name of Evan. I believe that together, with this information, we can make a difference to other traveling parents.

Since many airline employees (Reservation Agents, Unaccompanied Minor Supervisors, Gate Agents) as well as an Aviation Agent – all gave tips anonymously- I cannot name them. However, you know who you are—and I thank you!

Thank you to Travel Agents Kathryn and Bob, you both are kind people who make sure that parents aren't alone out there. Thank you for sharing what you have learned firsthand over a combined 77 years in the travel industry!

Thank you to Dr. Peter Contini, a well-respected board-certified pediatrician based in San Jose, California, who is a periodic guest on *The Ronn Owens KGO Radio* talk show. On the radio show, and in his practice, Peter Contini, M.D. often answers questions about travel, and he has 8 years of experience counseling parents on both domestic and international travel issues. His experience is not only as a pediatrician, but also as the father of three boys, ages 7, 4, and 2.

And of course, a big thank you to the wonderful traveling parents who are out there proving that it is possible and rewarding to fly with children. Many of them had to schedule late evening interviews after a full day with toddlers and once the kids were in bed!

- Gilly, a traveling mom
- Carole, commercial pilot and traveling mom of triplets
- Beth McGregor, traveling mom, private pilot and co-owner of a children's travel product website
- Brenda Elwell, traveling mom, single-parent travel expert, and owner of a single-parent travel website

Jet With Kids:
Taking the Fear Out of Flying
WITH YOUR KIDS!

16

- Louise Stoll, traveling grandma, inventor, owner of CARES harness website

I would also like to thank Captain Denny Fitch, Sr. for taking the time and patience to explain turbulence and some airplane terminology to me and all the other parents out there who are relying on this to make an informed decision about the safety of their most precious cargo. What you have accomplished in life is incredible and I am honored to have worked with you.

A thank you also to all of the fellow travelers I have spoken with in the airports, on planes and message boards, over the phone, and by e-mail. I appreciate everyone's willingness to contribute their time, and share their incredible experience in the traveling world in order to assist families as they introduce their children to the world of aviation transportation.

INTRODUCTION

I first flew as a toddler, and the flight was an international flight to Europe. My mom and I were flying to visit my grandparents in a small German village in the Black Forest. My mother had started her travels at a young age, leaving her home in Germany to live and work in Sweden as a private nurse for a physician's family. She came to America when she was 22 and continued her nursing career as a pediatric nurse at the Mayo Clinic hospital.

My youth is filled with memories of flights to Germany and Austria as well as going to the airport to pick up relatives visiting us from overseas. I have been to Europe nine times, four of those times as a child. For this I am forever grateful to my parents. They instilled a love of travel and seeing the world, and I learned that the world was bigger than my small hometown.

When I was 15, I asked my parents if we had any relatives on either coast. I contacted a great aunt on the East Coast and before I knew it, I was flying my first solo trip. My parents were shocked when, instead of being homesick after 2 weeks, I asked if I could stay longer since my cousins wanted to show me New York!

On another trip to Germany, I lived with my grandma for a summer. I visited "East" Germany and the still bomb-blackened city of Dresden shortly after the wall came down, the small, impoverished villages of the Czech Republic, and the amazing cathedrals in France.

I spent a summer in the Greek Islands, took a community nursing class in England, and met a German pen pal (in her hometown) whom I'd corresponded with since grade school.

Jet With Kids:
Taking the Fear Out of Flying
WITH YOUR KIDS!

18

I followed my mom's career steps and became a registered nurse at the Mayo Clinic. This only increased my hunger for travel since many of my patients were from all parts of the world. I learned some of my most valuable life lessons during that first year as a nurse.

The unit I worked on specialized in post surgical head and neck cancer patients, many of whom were diagnosed with serious, life-altering illnesses. These wonderful people came from all over the world to have the best care. From important dignitaries to Texas cowboys and even some Arab princes, they were truly a mix of the world's population.

I looked into their sad and scared, yet brave faces, as they would tell me about their poor prognosis or how this had forever changed their lifestyle. Their surgeries were drastic and shocking. To save them from the growing tumors, portions of their faces were removed and surgically reconstructed. None of them had thought something like this could or would ever happen to them.

The one thing I heard over and over was how they "wished they would have" done certain things in life. I remember one patient, Andrew, asking about my unusual name and where it came from. I replied that it was a popular German name. His reply will forever be in my mind and has guided me through life.

He said, "I always wanted to visit there. But you know how it is; I was waiting until I retired. I worked hard every day putting money into retirement so that my wife and I could travel someday. Now I may not make it that long. Anya, don't wait—there is never a *good* time to do things. LIVE your life, because it can be gone just like that."

> **I owe a lot to Andrew. From then on, if I wanted something,
> I made it happen.**

A few years later, living in California, I returned to my job at Mayo on a per diem basis, becoming the first RN to live in California and work at the Mayo Clinic in Minnesota. I would fly sometimes twice a month because I absolutely loved my job as a nurse there, and during a nationwide nursing shortage, I was able to fill in some needed hours.

(Little did I know at the time, the airline employees that I met and quickly became friends with on those flights and in the airports, would later be invaluable to me as I started the new adventure of parenting and traveling with a child.)

Jet With Kids:
Taking the Fear Out of Flying
WITH YOUR KIDS!

20

Chapter 1

You Can Fly With Kids

When I met my husband, our first conversation was about travel—and it has lasted over 10 years! My husband had also traveled quite often as a child and had the same thoughts about making travel a priority in life. We worked not to buy a bigger house or car or the latest clothes, but instead to fund that next trip, which we'd plan for months. We honeymooned in Germany and Switzerland. Over the years, we've traveled to Thailand, Malaysia, Australia, Mexico, Canada, the Caribbean Islands, Holland, Italy, England, Austria, France, Hawaii, Singapore, China and Japan. Many of these places we visited multiple times!

Before we got married, we had made a list of places in the world that we wanted to see, and we made it a goal to complete that list before we had children. Those around us had told us that we wouldn't be traveling when we had kids. I later discovered that these same people weren't big into traveling themselves, even without kids!

I was reminded of Andrew, my patient, when I met a couple in Thailand who told my husband and me—"Never, ever let others stop you. You can still travel with your children, and should, but *you will need to prepare and be ready for a different type of trip. Make it happen!"*

And that is exactly why my son had a passport at the age of 6 months and has already flown four times overseas and on multiple domestic flights!

At 17 months, my son hugged his great-grandmother in her small German village. He has played on the beautiful sandy beaches of Hawaii, San Diego, and Monterey. He has played with his cousins on the farm in the Midwest and actually learned those animal noises from real live animals instead of just a book. He has played with a little Austrian boy at the Christmas Market in Salzburg and has eaten gelato with a little Italian girl in Rome.

> **I had never truly experienced the local culture
> as much as when we traveled with our son.**

Not only did he have international playmates, the local people —who had so many times before looked right past me—were now smiling at him or starting conversations with me. Sharing this travel with my son was also a great opening into people's lives. The Italian gelato was given so freely just for a smile or a chance to interact with us. The Hawaiians presented beautiful flower leis to my son with a smile expressing love for children and a welcome to the store we were in.

These are just a very few of the things that I had walked right past in my previous travels. Yes, it was a much easier trip for me on the surface before I had children, but I can honestly say that traveling with children really breaks all barriers and allows you to see the locals for who they really are—caring, kind, and oftentimes parents themselves!

All of these fabulous experiences started out with – the flight!

As we have all learned as parents, the more prepared and flexible we can be, the better things go. I can't emphasize this enough when it comes to airline travel with children.

> **You don't have to be a seasoned traveler
> to do well and enjoy your family trip!**

I do a lot of research when I plan trips. So my first trip as a parent was going to be no different. I was determined to travel and have a great time. So I started to research the first step of the journey, which was the flight, and I realized that there is a lot of great information out there, but it took me hours to pull it all together. (And we all know there are never enough hours available to parents!) I also found that the best insights I got were the ones from all those gate agents, pilots, traveling moms, and flight attendants whom I had met over the years.

I decided to put all that advice together. At first, it was just for my friends and myself. Then I realized that if *we* had these questions, surely other new parents or novice travelers did too! I began looking at the message boards on the Internet, and they were filled with the same questions over and over. I contacted all my "airline friends," and found that even though many were underpaid and overworked, their love of travel and understanding of the challenges of flying with children brought out an enthusiasm that was contagious.

I am proud to present you with the **ultimate resource** for flying with children. My experience was limited compared to these travel professionals—I formally interviewed 21 people. Their travel and experience flying with children totals over 450 years!

> These people have seen it all—from the sobering realization of lessons learned in a fiery plane crash, to the traveling insights of a mother who has been to 67 countries, taking her children to half of them as a *single* parent.

Congratulations on taking the next step to showing your children the world. I hope to make it a pleasant trip for all!

Compiling This Book

Some of you are preparing for your first trip with a child, and others are trying to make sure there are no repeats of the disaster that was the first trip. I applaud you all for taking the time to do your homework. Is it easy traveling with a child? Not compared to sipping champagne in first class as a young woman with only herself and her husband to think about! However, I can honestly say that I love to travel with my son.

It was wonderful talking to these travel experts since they all gave their honest, heartfelt answers. They truly did want to make the process easier for parents—many of them being parents themselves.

These wonderful people have shared their stories and advice, hoping to make the flight process easier for parents and children and believing that an educated parent is a better-prepared passenger.

I am more convinced than ever that these special people do their jobs out of love for travel and definitely not for pay. I was horrified to hear personal stories of huge pay cuts, downsizing, and increasing workloads. While I was writing this, a few of them were out looking for work having received notice that their 25-year long jobs were being eliminated in the near future. Some of them were working three jobs to make ends meet. I realized then that both the airlines and the public sorely under appreciate them.

Almost all of the people I interviewed are parents themselves, and some are even grandparents.

> **This understanding of how unpredictable the airlines and even children can be, combined with decades of experience, and an enthusiasm for travel helped to make this an unbelievable resource.**

Jet With Kids:
Taking the Fear Out of Flying
WITH YOUR KIDS!

24

I am including links to airline policies on certain topics, however for the everyday tips, I wanted more than just policies to offer you. I wanted to hear from those at the "ground level." For that reason, most of the information has been given anonymously, and with great honesty. No specific airline or currently employed airline employee is named.

Chapter 2

Using a Travel Agent

I have found that for the traveling parent especially, it is many times beneficial to have your own travel advocate. Your personal travel agent is someone who keeps up with the policies, who will be your representative in times of a canceled flight, or a need for rescheduling. An experienced travel agent is an incredible asset and will learn your preferences and cut through all of the headaches for you.

As a parent with limited time, think how nice it would be to call your agent with your needs and be assured that your booking will be done professionally. Working with the same person allows you to build a relationship over the years. As you work with an agent, this person will get to know your likes, dislikes, and preferences. You can rely on your agent to serve you with integrity.

Airlines are becoming more automated, and you may be faced with a computer kiosk and only one phone at the counter to deal with the questions and concerns of 150 other passengers.

> **How nice would it be to call your personal agent and relax, knowing that everything is taken care of?**

Check out the link below from Fodors, a popular travel guide. The article lists instances when using a travel agent is especially beneficial.
http://www.fodors.com/wire/archives/001963.cfm

Jet With Kids:
Taking the Fear Out of Flying
WITH YOUR KIDS!

26

I had the opportunity to interview two travel agents with great experience to share with families. Let me introduce them:

Kathryn W. Sudeikis, CTC
ALL ABOUT TRAVEL
5331 Johnson Drive
Mission, Kansas 66205
Tel: 913-671-7700 ▪ 800-999-5344 ext. 325
E-mail: KSudeikis@aatusa.com
Website: http://www.AllAboutTravelUSA.com
Travel tips: http://www.travelsense.org

Who is Kathryn W. Sudeikis, CTC?

PAST PRESIDENT – AMERICAN SOCIETY OF TRAVEL AGENTS

Kathryn W. Sudeikis, CTC, vice president of corporate relations for All About Travel in Mission, Kansas, a suburb of Kansas City, Missouri, was inducted as ASTA's National President and Chief Executive Office in October 2004. Previously, Sudeikis served two terms as national vice president and two years as the national secretary.

A working travel agent, Sudeikis appeared in 2002, 2003, 2004, 2005 and 2006 editions of Travel and Leisure magazine as one of their "Super Travel Agent" recommendations to their readers. She was featured with her specialty of intergenerational family travel. Also in 2002, Sudeikis was recognized as "Travel Agent of the Year" by the readers of Travel Trade magazine.

In 2005, Sudeikis was awarded a Lifetime Achievement Award from Travel Weekly and was nominated as "Outstanding Industry Association Executive" by the World Travel Awards.

A 35-year industry veteran, Sudeikis is frequently quoted in national publications, including the Kansas City newspapers, The Chicago Tribune, Washington Post, Wall Street Journal, Los Angeles Times and USA TODAY. She has appeared on numerous national television programs including FOX News, "The News Hour with Jim Lehrer," "The Today Show" and "CBS This Morning." She has also appeared on several radio programs, including National Public Radio, Radio Free Europe and the Armed Forces Radio Network

An accomplished speaker, Sudeikis has addressed groups at many industry events, including the National Tour Association (NTA), the Travel Industry Association of America (TIA), the Cruise Lines International Association (CLIA) and the Travel Agent Associations of India, South Africa, Australia and Germany.

Sudeikis earned her Certified Travel Counselor (CTC) distinction in 1976 from The Travel Institute (formerly the Institute of Certified Travel Agents) and was awarded a lifetime membership in 1983. She has served on Travel Agent Advisory Boards for Classic Vacation, the German National Tourist Office, Rail Europe and Thrifty Car Rental.

Before her national election Sudeikis was a member of ASTA's Board of Directors representing the Missouri Valley and Upper Midwest Chapters. Sudeikis was the chairman of ASTA's 1993 World Travel Congress. The annual Congress, which attracts thousands of travel agents and travel suppliers from around the world, is the Society's largest event. Sudeikis has also served the Society as presiding officer of ASTA's Chapter Presidents Council, and as a member of the Public Relations Committee and the Aviation Committee. She has appeared in Travel Agent magazine's "100 Most Powerful Women" in 1999-2002.

As the chairman of ASTA's Future Planning Committee, she led a taskforce responsible for developing ASTA's new category of individual membership. Prior to that, Sudeikis was the lead issue manager on ASTA's consumer awareness campaign. Sudeikis oversaw the Society's efforts to promote the value of the travel agent and spearheaded the public relations campaign, with the slogan, "Without a travel agent, you're on your own."

About ASTA

The mission of the American Society of Travel Agents and its affiliate organizations is to enhance the professionalism and profitability of members worldwide through effective representation in industry and government affairs, education and training, and by identifying and meeting the needs of the traveling public. The Society is the world's largest and most influential travel trade association with 20,000 members in more than 140 countries.

Here Kathryn describes what it means to have a personal travel agent:

> *It's about the relationship, and when you've got somebody in your back pocket, somebody who is like a florist that you don't need all the time but you want one you love and you know does a good job. You want a caterer if you're going to throw a party, you want a plumber you trust, you want a tax accountant you trust, and that's how the relationship with the travel agent should be. We're just another tool in your tool basket that you don't have to interview and start over with every time you want to use one.* (Kathryn Sudeikis, CTC - Travel Agent, 35 years experience)

Here are some tips that Kathryn recommends for finding a good travel agent for your family's needs:

Jet With Kids:
Taking the Fear Out of Flying
WITH YOUR KIDS!

28

1. Ask someone you trust to recommend a travel agent.

2. Look for professional credentials such as CTC (Certified Travel Counselor), CTA (Certified Travel Associate), or DS (Destination Specialist).

3. Look for a company that is a member of the American Society of Travel Agents. This ensures that you have a consumer-affairs department to respond to any unacceptable situations you may have with your travel agent (http://www.astanet.com).

> *You ask someone if they use a travel agent. If they have a travel agent they love, they will tell you over and over and over about what they've done for them. So that is one of the first places to turn to find someone. Then you look for someone who has credentials behind their name, like I have a CTC (Certified Travel Counselor), because it is a personal designation. And then you look for a company that's a member of the American Society of Travel Agents because if something does go wrong you have a recourse and a consumer affairs department that would run interference for you if you had any unacceptable situation if someone didn't solve a problem for you, for example.* (Kathryn Sudeikis, CTC- Travel Agent, 35 years experience)

4. You may want to look for a family travel specialist.

5. The industry has changed a lot in the last 5 years; it is okay to work with an agent who works only online and doesn't have a brick-and-mortar business.

Some words of caution from Kathryn:

• Make sure the agent is not *telling* you what to do, but is *asking* lots of questions.

- Never make a check out to a travel agent; always use a credit card to protect yourself, and if you're writing a check, make it out only to the corporation.

Bob Robar

Travel Centre
4061-20 NW 43 Street
Gainesville, FL 32606
Tel: **1-800-881-2218** ▪ E-mail: bob@travelcentre.com

Who is Bob Robar?

Bob's experience in the travel industry extends over the past 42 years! He worked for Eastern Airlines for 25 years in various customer service positions, mainly at the ticket counter, becoming Chief Agent in Gainesville, Florida. He also worked gates, baggage service, flight operations, flight ramp service, aircraft cleaning, and travel agency sales. When Eastern filed for bankruptcy in 1991, Bob formed a travel agency and has owned two agencies since then, at one time employing eight employees.

His present company, Travel Centre of Gainesville, was chosen as one of the top two travel agencies in Florida in 1999. He is on the Board of Directors of his ASTA (American Society of Travel Agents) chapter. He is a board member and is past President of his local Rotary Club and Vice President of the North American Rotary Fellowship of Travel Agents.

> *We are the agent for the customer, so if there's any issues or any problems or anything like that, you've got somebody you can come back to with a face other than an electronic identification number somewhere on an Internet site. We've had customers . . . call on their cell and say, 'My flight's canceled and the lines are 3 miles long. What can I do?' We pull up the computer and book them on a new flight and they just get out of line and go get on another flight.* (Bob Robar, Travel Agent, 42 years experience)

Jet With Kids:
Taking the Fear Out of Flying
WITH YOUR KIDS!

30

Bob states that when you use a travel agent, there is non biased booking (it doesn't list one airline over another, it is possible for the agent to see what the airline agent sees on their screen, and they can get last-minute availability).

Our computers are literally exactly what the airline agent sees on their screen. (Bob Robar, Travel Agent, 42 years experience)

Chapter 3

Traveling during Pregnancy

You may be a frequent flier, but once you are pregnant, all sorts of doubts and questions come into mind about the safety of flying and the pregnant mom. I can remember the research I did when I was pregnant. I had planned a trip to Tokyo and Singapore for the Fall of 2003. At the time of booking, I had no plans for pregnancy and definitely no idea that I would be 10 weeks pregnant and very nauseated when this trip to Asia actually occurred!

> *I panicked - was it okay to travel internationally when I was pregnant?*

I received conflicting advice, and once again, I found that the people who were warning me against travel did not make travel a priority for themselves. There are extra precautions to take, of course. For example, now that I was pregnant I would not be eating some of the things in Tokyo that I had envisioned when planning the trip in the first place.

I was also a typical first-time mother in that I didn't just believe people when they said, "Oh you will be fine—just don't travel when you are in labor."

I like to be in the middle, traveling as a pregnant mom, but taking precautions to maintain the health of my unborn child and myself.

Airline Policies Regarding Travel during Pregnancy

Some airlines are more lax than others about how far into your pregnancy you may be and still be allowed to travel. The following link lists the policies of major domestic airlines:

http://www.babycenter.com/general/pregnancytravel/pregnancy/6976.html.

> **Most airlines do not allow you to fly domestically past 36 weeks or internationally past 32 weeks due to fear of an onboard delivery.**

Always check with your obstetrician before flying. I recommend bringing a simple letter signed by your physician, stating your due date and that you are cleared for travel. It is also a good idea to bring along your medical records and insurance card when traveling. (As you would with any confidential information, protect this and be responsible for keeping it in your possession.)

 # Flight Tips

If you're pregnant I would get an aisle seat, get your doctor's okay no matter how far along you are. Move around [and wear] comfortable clothing. (Gate Agent Victoria, 23 years experience)

Here are some other great tips:
1. Pregnancy increases chances of DVTs (Deep Vein Thrombosis), also known as blood clots, in the legs and pelvis, due to changes in the circulatory system. This risk increases with prolonged sitting and dehydration (both occur with flying). *In addition to reading the tips below, see "What you can do to prevent travel-related DVTs" (p. 142)

a. <u>Stay hydrated</u>. Avoid drinking coffee and alcoholic beverages, as they may cause you to lose fluids and increase dehydration. Increase your water intake. Purchase water after security to take onboard; don't rely on the airline to supply enough.

b. <u>Avoid sitting for long periods of time</u>. Some travelers find standing (only when seat belt sign is turned off), walking the aisle (sitting in an aisle seat makes this easier), and performing simple leg exercises in your seat (flexing leg and calf muscles, rotating ankles, pointing toes) to be helpful.

c. <u>Some travelers find wearing compression stockings helpful</u> (available at most pharmacies). Hospitals routinely have post surgery patients wear these in the hospital to prevent blood from pooling in their legs and causing DVTs.

2. <u>Avoid carbonated beverages and gas-producing foods the day before flying</u>. Indigestion is common in pregnancy and becomes more pronounced while flying. As the plane ascends, air pressure decreases, and the gases in your intestines expand. With pregnancy comes slower digestion. More gas accumulates and gives you a bloated, uncomfortable feeling that can make you miserable. (As a nurse, I witnessed sometimes the most severe pain in post surgical patients being not the incision, but gas pain)!

3. <u>Avoid eating high-sodium foods the day before you fly</u>. You will retain fluid and increase the swelling in your legs.

4. <u>Consider taking a seat close to the bathroom</u>. If you have nausea and feel like vomiting, you can get to the bathroom quickly. However, unpleasant odors can be strong near the bathroom.

5. <u>If you have morning sickness and are nauseous</u>, here are a couple products that may help to alleviate your symptoms:

Discomfort Wrist Band & Queasy Pops:
http://www.JetWithKidsClub.com/health

> *I had morning sickness the first 14 weeks of my*
> *pregnancy, and was headed to Tokyo at 10 weeks, worried*
> *about the nausea. I tried everything I could find,*
> *including the two items above. I also drank a ton of water*
> *and carried a handkerchief with a pleasing smell of essential oil on it to*
> *use in case an odor started to get to me. (I was extremely sensitive to*
> *odors and being in close proximity to strangers – and their body odor or*
> *breath - on the plane made me nervous!) I can't say exactly what helped,*
> *but the combination of these things really helped and my morning*
> *sickness was not an issue! (Anya's review)*

6.   Bring a pillow along for comfort (behind lower back, to lean against, etc.).

7.   Wear loose, comfortable clothing and shoes. Swelling of the feet is common during pregnancy due to increased dilation of the blood vessels. Prolonged sitting will make this worse, so wear loose but supportive shoes. (I took my shoes off once on a flight and was unable to fit the same shoes back on at the end of the flight – this swelling with flying and pregnancy does happen!)

8.   Do not be afraid to ask someone to assist you with lifting your luggage. A pleasant attitude, smile, and gratitude go a long way!

Chapter 4

Traveling with a Newborn

I have seen many first-time parents traveling with tiny babies, many times in order to introduce their new little one to the extended family in other areas of the world.

> **This is a double adventure for the first-time parents, since they are also getting used to being parents!**

As one experienced flight attendant notes about new parents, *New parents are very self-conscious that their child's fussing or crying a little bit. I like to reassure them . . . they might be a little fussy or the time change is making them out of sorts, just to relax a little bit; everybody's had a crying baby before. I think when the parents are upset, their kids can feel it.* (Flight Attendant A, 28 years experience)

 Safe Age to Travel

I asked Peter Contini M.D. when parents could plan to travel for the first time with a newborn.

Generally what I recommend, for brief travel, say 2 hours or less, they can pretty much take their child whenever they want to. Once you get beyond that, and particularly when you're flying internationally, I prefer that patients wait until a minimum of 2 months of age so they've at least received their first set of immunizations, and any other congenital problems will have by then usually shown

Jet With Kids:
Taking the Fear Out of Flying
WITH YOUR KIDS!

36

themselves and you'll know about them. (Peter Contini, M.D., 8 years experience)

Always check with your airline to confirm their minimum age requirements.

 ## Comfort on the Plane

Remember that the temperature can be cooler on flights. It is always a good idea to bring along a blanket for children. This can be used for many different things and always comes in handy when trying to breastfeed a baby near strangers!

Chapter 5

Keeping Your Family Healthy for the Flight

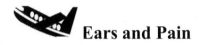 **Ears and Pain**

Ear pressure—Peter Contini, M.D. believes this issue is usually overblown, and problems with ear pressure don't happen as frequently as most travelers think. But when ear pain does occur, it can be excruciating. Since I have actually felt the ear pain in past flights, I wanted Dr. Contini to explain what is actually happening. Parents are told to have their child suck on something, but no further explanation is usually offered. Here is a great explanation from Dr. Contini:

> *Essentially what happens is contraction of air during landing causes a vacuum and pulling on the eardrum and it can cause pain. What sucking does, same thing as crying can do it, yawning can do it, chewing gum if you're an adult can do it, chewing on anything really can do it; what it would do is it would actually move and wiggle the Eustachian tube and allow it to release some of the pressure that's built up behind the ear, and that allows the ear drum to then normalize again.* (Peter Contini, M.D., 8 years experience)

When the flight attendants walk through the cabin, checking passenger seat belts in preparation for landing or if the pilot announces the start of the descent, begin to feed your child. Swallowing will help equalize the pressure in the ears during descent.

Find out more information about the effects of altitude on ears from the American Academy of Otolaryngology Head and Neck Surgery: http://www.entnet.org/healthinfo/ears/altitude.cfm

Flight Attendant Karen (29 years of experience) writes the following about a product available for children:
"Earplanes: a product for children to help with ear discomfort when flying. These special earplugs tightly seal, therefore slowing down rapid pressure changes that affect the ear."

Earplanes:
http://www.JetWithKidsClub.com/health

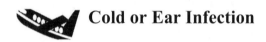 ## Cold or Ear Infection

Please consult with your physician when your child is sick to make sure he is well enough to fly. Peter Contini, M.D. stated that when a child has a cold or ear infection, studies have shown that decongestants are not very helpful or effective for kids. Fluids and TLC are good.

 ## Teething

If your baby or toddler is teething, take this into consideration when planning your trip. This can be very painful for some babies, and your flight could feel a lot longer just by overlooking these small comfort measures. Bring along teething rings (can be put in a cup with ice to keep them cold), teething gel, or pain medication approved by your pediatrician. **Always consult with your physician before administering supplements or medications to your child to ensure that there are no contraindications.**

General Health Tips

Follow these general health tips to keep your family healthy before and during the trip.

1. Try to limit the exposure of your child to other little children the week before you travel. Many illnesses will show up days after exposure, and a sick child who is in a weakened state of immunity, irritable, and needing rest is definitely a contraindication for flying.

2. Avoid sugar and junk food.

3. Motion Sickness: Keep in mind the possibility of motion sickness in your children. Due to excitement/stress make sure that your child does not eat too much before or during your flight. The combination of an overfull stomach and nervousness combined with motion and turbulence can be disastrous for all involved! There are a couple over the counter products that may help to alleviate symptoms of motion sickness (consult with your family physician first before using these products)

Discomfort Wrist Bands and Queasy Pops:
http://www.JetWithKidsClub.com/health

4. Encourage thorough hand washing with soap to prevent the spread of germs. Beth McGregor of Traveling With Kids describes some popular products for minimizing germs.
4-in-1 Germ Protector
(**http://www.JetWithKidsClub.com/health**) a place mat that can be used on the airplane to cover up tray, and cover child's lap as well.

Public Potty Protectors
(**http://www.JetWithKidsClub.com/health**) falls over the side of the toilet so child is not touching a dirty toilet.

Jet With Kids:
Taking the Fear Out of Flying
WITH YOUR KIDS!

40

Germ Patrol Quick Dry Surface Sanitizer
(**http://www.JetWithKidsClub.com/health**) apply to
tray in airplane to seal and protect from germs.

Air Right Personal Air Purification
(**http://www.JetWithKidsClub.com/health**) attach to the
overhead air nozzle to remove pollutants from your personal
airspace.

5.   If you are planning on administering any medication that is new to
a child, try it out at home first.

6.   Bring a small first-aid kit along. There are a couple different ones
available for kids:

First Aid Kit
(**http://www.JetWithKidsClub.com/health**)

Pedia Pak First Aid Kit
(**http://www.JetWithKidsClub.com/health**) : a nurse
and her pediatrician developed this when she, as a mom
traveling to Russia to pick up her adopted baby, didn't find
what she was looking for–so she created what she needed!

Chapter 6

What You Need to Know about the Lap Child

 The Lap Child Policy

As a general rule, a child under the age of 2 is allowed to travel as a "lap child." This does not always mean "free." On international flights you are charged a "small" fee for bringing a lap child, but by the time fuel surcharges and taxes are added in, it can cost over $250. *And you still have to hold your child!*

All airlines have different policies and practices when it comes to the lap child. What I thought about the lap child before I started writing this has drastically changed since digging into the research. To be honest, I had not given it as much thought as I should have. When deciding whether or not to buy a seat, I usually thought about how convenient it was relative to cost and our budget. I am thankful when I look back, that those flights when my son was on my lap went without incident. However, now that I have read the facts and heard the stories, I am horrified that a lap child is even an option.

> I guess that because the option was there, I had assumed it meant that the FAA and the airlines thought it was *safe* for him to be on my lap. That is quite the opposite of the truth!

Take a look at some of the links that demonstrate this point:

The **Federal Aviation Administration** explains the importance of securing children in a child restraint system, stating, "Did you know the safest place for your little one during turbulence or

Jet With Kids:
Taking the Fear Out of Flying
WITH YOUR KIDS!

42

an emergency is in an approved child restraint system (CRS), not on your lap?"

http://www.faa.gov/passengers/fly_children/crs/

> **The FAA mission statement says their "mission is to provide the safest, most efficient, aerospace system in the world. . . . Our vision is to improve the safety and efficiency of aviation, while being responsive to our customers and accountable to the public. . . . Safety is our passion"**
> **(http://www.FAA.gov/about/mission).**

The FAA states that it is NOT safe to hold your child on your lap. They even have a campaign to educate parents. I, for one, had never seen these ads before I started digging through research.

http://www.faa.gov/passengers/media/7X10ARMS.pdf
http://www.faa.gov/passengers/media/childsafety.pdf
http://www.faa.gov/passengers/media/RADIO_scripts.pdf

Safe Ride News offers a resource website for health and safety professionals. "The goals of Safe Ride News Publications are to help save lives and prevent injury to children in traffic." The link that follows explains the importance of using a car seat on the plane, lists which car seats are allowed on planes, and gives suggestions for preparing to fly with a car seat.

http://saferidenews.com/html/Airplane_Eng.htm

> **NO ONE says it is safe for your child to be a lap child.**

In 2001, the **American Academy of Pediatrics** came out very strongly in favor of child restraints:
http://aappolicy.aappublications.org/cgi/content/full/pediatrics%3b108/5/1218

The **American Academy of Pediatrics** states that there have been preventable injuries and deaths in survivable crashes and turbulence due to children under 2 not being properly restrained in an aircraft. This link is an abstract summarizing their statements. http://www.ncbi.nlm.nih.gov/entrez/query.fcgi?cmd=retrieve&db=pubmed&list_uids=11694707&dopt=Abstract

The required use of child-restraint systems for children under two is listed on the **NTSB's (National Transportation Safety Board)** list of most-wanted transportation safety improvements. http://www.ntsb.gov/recs/mostwanted/aircraft_child_restraints.htm

NADA (National Air Disaster Alliance)

Stephanie Manus, a survivor of a plane crash in Arkansas, urges parents to purchase a seat. Her letter to parents also includes a note that can be sent directly to the FAA, urging them to take the necessary steps to mandate seat belts for children under 2. Refer to the link below to read Stephanie's letter.

http://www.planesafe.org/safety/saferchildren.htm

Everyone concerned with your child's safety states that it is safest for your child to be restrained during flight.

I was told by numerous airline reservation agents that I did not need to buy a seat and actually was discouraged from doing so. I wish they could listen to the following radio ad from the FAA, and then explain to me what is safe about holding my child as a lap child.

Furthermore, I would like the FAA to tell parents the truth and demand that the airlines warn them of the dangers of a lap child. Listen to this radio ad that has lullaby music playing in the background as a woman's soft voice describes your precious baby and how she looks in your arms. Her voice takes on a threatening, horror-filled tone as she tells you that you can never hold a baby tight enough to protect her on an airplane. She states that unexpected turbulence does happen and basically that <u>if you want to hold on to your baby for a lifetime, a safety seat is the best place for her on an airplane.</u>

<u>http://www.faa.gov/passengers/media/Track01.mp3</u>

The FAA is, in effect, relieving itself of responsibility by creating these ads. I would understand their purpose more if these ads were significantly posted in airports and airlines were required to also share this information with you. However, every single person that I talked to had never heard of these ads. And they all were *frequent flying* parents!

So, if EVERYONE that has safety of the child in mind states that holding a child on your lap is not safe, then why is it not mandatory to have the child restrained like everyone over 2 years old? Why am I as a parent given the option to choose to disregard the safety of my infant—just because of his age?

> **If the FAA and airlines give me, as a parent,
> the option to hold my baby in my arms while flying 500 miles per hour, then
> they should make sure I'm educated about the truth and the dangers so that
> I am able to make an informed decision.**

The reassurances the airline reservations agents gave for holding my infant as a lap child ranged from "everyone does it" and "sure it's safe" to "you shouldn't buy a seat because your baby will sleep better in your arms." After the research I've done, I'm convinced they shouldn't be saying those things.

FAA Response

The FAA states that they do not want to turn people away from flying and toward driving, due to the increased cost of purchasing a ticket for their child. Because of a higher rate of automobile accidents, that child would be at a higher risk on more dangerous highways and in fact be in more danger than on a plane. www.faa.gov/news/press_releases/news_story.cfm?contentkey=1966

> **This made me wonder why it is not mandatory to purchase a seat on overseas flights where driving is not an option.**

Everyone else and everything else on a plane needs to be secured during takeoff, landing, and in the event of turbulence. A pet in a carrier under the seat, a laptop, and carry-on luggage all have to be secured. Yet, a child in the arms of a parent is not AT ALL protected when it comes to planes that are going 500 miles per hour! OR if the takeoff is aborted suddenly on the runway at 120 miles per hour. Why is it mandatory that every other human being and ITEM is secured, and not precious infants?

Jan Brown-Lohr Interview:

There is nothing as sobering as talking to someone who has been through a plane crash and walked out a survivor. I became especially convinced of the importance of purchasing a seat for an infant after interviewing Jan Brown-Lohr, the Chief Flight Attendant in the 1989 crash of a DC10. You can feel the emotion and horror that she faced when she looked into the eyes of the mother of little 22-month-old Evan, who was a lap child that did not survive the crash. Jan realized that day that the instructions to put your child on the floor to protect him sounded plausible in the classroom setting, but were absolutely ludicrous when faced with a real-life emergency.

Read this statement that Jan made as she represented the Association of Flight Attendants at the NTSB Advocacy Briefing on Child Restraints on Aircraft in February of 2004: http://ashsd.afacwa.org/docs/Jan%20Lohr%20NTSB%20Brief.pdf

Following is the tragic story of the horrific crash of United Flight 232 in Sioux City, Iowa as told to me by Retired Chief Flight Attendant, Jan Brown-Lohr:

Jet With Kids:
Taking the Fear Out of Flying
WITH YOUR KIDS!

46

There were 4 lap children on board the flight that day. One of the mother's had told Jan that she was specifically taking the flight to take advantage of a free flight for her son who was 22 months. (Current airline policy allows children up to 24 months to sit on their parent's lap for free –they are known as "lap children" and are not buckled in or restrained)

The DC-10 lost all hydraulics and flight control, and a crash landing was imminent. Jan prepared the passengers on how to get into the brace position.

As Jan had learned in emergency preparedness training, she instructed the parents of the lap children to place their children on the floor at their feet and lean over them. Jan relates with a tear-filled voice that to this day it makes her skin crawl that she had to tell parents to put their most precious possessions on the floor and hold them down.

The plane crashed with such force that it split into 3 sections. Jan's section of the plane (as well as the section of the parents with the 22-month old) turned over and was upside down in a cornfield next to the runway.

The first person Jan encountered outside of the plane was the mother of the 22-month old. She was going back to the plane to look for her child, Evan. Jan told her she couldn't go back. The mother looked at her and said that Jan had told her to put the baby on the floor and now he was gone.

Jan will always feel the pain and horror of losing that child. The G-forces were so strong, there was no way a child could be held, and he was killed.

Jan has worked these past 17 years as an advocate of children's safety. She will speak out until ALL children are required to be restrained on airplanes.

Jan has been doing interviews, has testified in Congress twice, has started e-mail campaigns, and has been educating the public for the past 17 years. She has felt it her purpose to be the voice of Evan. She will continue to speak out until the regulations are changed and **everyone** is required to be safely restrained in a seat for all flights.

As Jan states, *"Parents wouldn't dream of driving 50–60 miles per hour in a car on the highway without their child being buckled in. Yet they will put their baby in a metal tube that goes 500 miles per hour unrestrained."*

Like I said earlier, I am a very protective mother and my first concern is always for the safety of my son.

> **Yet, I allowed him to be a lap child, because I was under the impression that the FAA, with its role for keeping passengers safe in airplanes, would not allow an unsafe policy.**

There is a poignant video of the United Airlines accident where at the time, they said to the parents, the best way (to secure) your child was to put them down on the floor and you lean over them and hold them instead of buckling them in, and 2 of the children just shot off like missiles. (Flight Attendant A, 28 years experience)

> **All passengers are in danger of being injured when there is even one lap child on board.**

A child's weight multiplies up to and more than 5 times their normal weight and that's why they'll go off like a bullet and that's why people don't realize; anybody sitting in a cabin with a lap child is at risk. Because if that child goes off like a bullet and it hits somebody, can you imagine what 100 pounds or more is going to do to the person it connects with? (Jan Brown-Lohr, Retired Flight Attendant, 25 years experience)

What can we as parents do to urge the FAA to change its regulations? An organized group of parents would be a powerful group, and the FAA/airlines want to keep the traveling family as a consumer. Jan recommends that we encourage the FAA by e-mail to listen to our concerns about the lap child option. She states: *"The FAA would be the agency to besiege with e-mail regarding child seats, since in the*

Jet With Kids:
Taking the Fear Out of Flying
WITH YOUR KIDS!

48

end they are the agency responsible for mandating child restraints on planes." The head of the FAA is Marion Blakey and her e-mail contact is marion.blakey@faa.gov.

If you would like, you can copy this note in an e-mail to her.

Dear Marion:

As a concerned parent/grandparent/traveler, I am writing today to strongly encourage the FAA to mandate child restraints for children under two on airplanes. I believe that the lap child option is a danger to children as well as every other passenger sitting on an aircraft. In the event of severe turbulence or a crash, NOBODY is safe when an object of any kind or an infant is free to propel through the cabin. I expect the FAA, as an advocate of airline safety, to enforce policies that will protect those who utilize airplanes as a way of transport, regardless of age.

Sincerely,
Your name and address and any additional comments

**The airlines are responsible for getting passengers from point A to point B.
Parents are responsible for their children and
making informed decisions to keep their children safe.
The FAA is responsible for mandating aviation safety.... so why doesn't that
include protecting children under two years old?**

The same day that I interviewed Jan, *The New York Times* published an online article discussing the issue of child restraint seats for airplanes. The article, written by Michael Decourcy Hinds, states, "Given the F.A.A. policy, travelers may have assumed that unrestrained children face little safety risk on aircraft. In fact, an unrestrained passenger of any age faces a higher risk of death or injury in a survivable crash or severe turbulence than passengers who are strapped into safety seats or belts" (*New York Times*, August 24, 2006).
http://query.nytimes.com/gst/fullpage.html?sec=travel&res=9503E0D
D1F38F93BA2575BC0A963948260

The decision to allow a lap child was made to prevent you from choosing driving over flying—not because it is safe for your child. I do understand that many people are budget conscious and yes, it does cost more money for an additional seat. On average, the estimated additional cost would be $200 per family. However, have you ever heard a police officer say, "Well I understand that you cannot afford a car seat, so it is okay not to buckle up your child"?

Why does the smallest, most dependent person in the family get the least protection? Is it really a choice of IF you should buckle your child in and fly safely with them?

I think that once you consider what you are risking, the cost of a seat for each and every one of your children becomes part of the budget. It is also interesting to me that on many of the message boards, mothers are asking, "Should I buy a seat or is it unnecessary?" The question is not that it will make the trip financially unattainable. I think many parents assume like I did that if taking a lap child is an option then it must be safe. And most parents are concerned with their child's safety above and beyond anything else. In severe turbulence ask a parent what they would pay to buckle their child in and be able to offer their child the same protection that they themselves have.

Thinking that you as a parent can hold your child as securely as a seat belt is not realistic. And how much of the time on that flight are you actually holding that baby securely? Babies will play on the floor, sit on your lap, and sometimes snuggle while both of you sleep. This happened to my son and me on a 5-hour flight. I am embarrassed to admit that I—a safety freak normally—fell asleep with my hand casually on my son's stomach. You may plan to be good about holding them securely, but 5 hours is a long time. Even two hours is long with a toddler . . . The reality is that you are not going to secure that child for an entire flight like a seat belt would.

Even though a child under two may sit on an adult's lap for takeoff and landing, it is not safe for the child to travel in this manner. After United Airlines DC10 lost hydraulic power and crashed into an

Jet With Kids:
Taking the Fear Out of Flying
WITH YOUR KIDS!

50

Iowa corn field many summers ago, flight attendants have been lobbying the government to make sure all children are kept safe by being properly restrained during the critical phases of flight. United Airlines flight attendants recounted the fact that all the infants in that crash were not restrained by the adults that were holding them. (The force of impact is just too great.) ...It is still an option whether or not to buy a seat for a child under two but most parents do not understand what a dangerous situation this can be. (Flight Attendant Karen, 29 years of experience)

My goal is not to tell you what to do.
My intent is to educate you so that your decision can be an informed one.
Your child's safety is ultimately
YOUR responsibility.
Your children depend on YOU
to take care of their needs and keep them safe.

Critics will say plane crashes are rare and ask, "What are the chances that anyone would survive a crash anyway?" My answer is that the danger with these unsecured babies is not just the crash; it is also the unexpected turbulence. And two of the people I interviewed for this resource were plane crash survivors – who not only survived, but went on to make an incredible difference in many people's lives.

The danger with these unsecured babies is not just the crash;
it is also the unexpected turbulence.

 **Turbulence**

http://www.aviationspeakers.com/Speakers/denny-fitch.php

We have all felt a bit of turbulence at some time or another when flying. Sometimes being more severe than others, it is often just thought of as being annoying. However, as I have done more and more research on the dangers of the lap child, many flight attendants warned me of the issues of turbulence and especially the unexpected clear air turbulence that has been known in the past to cause injuries and even has been fatal for lap children.

These incidents are not very well known, and it is interesting that there is not any place for these injuries to be documented. I know that many people comment on the slim possibilities of a crash occurring when defending the lap child policy. I was interested in finding out more about the danger of *turbulence* that the FAA refers to in many of its ads, warning of the dangers of an unrestrained child.

As with every other topic in this resource, I consulted with an expert. I was honored to be able to interview Captain Denny Fitch, Sr., a pilot who was instrumental in saving 184 lives in the incredible DC-10 crash landing of United Airlines Flight 232 in Sioux City, Iowa. His unique experience of crash landing a jet without hydraulics and flight control, and acting courageously through every pilot's worst nightmare, earned him Presidential and Congressional Honors, as well as a place in the Aviation Hall of Fame.

His experience speaks for itself:
- 7 years as an Air Force pilot
- 34 years in the airlines; Captain at United Airlines; DC-10 flight instructor; check airman
- Accumulated over 20,000 hours of flight time
- President of his own Aviation Consulting Firm
- Safety Consultant to NASA – a member of the Aerospace Safety Advisory Panel
- Inducted into the Aviation Hall of Fame at the Smithsonian National Air and Space Museum
- Commended by President George Bush and was given Congressional Honor for his involvement in the emergency landing of the DC-10 without hydraulics or flight control
- Along with the rest of the crew, he holds the distinguished record of longest time aloft without flight controls who lived to tell about it.
- Motivational and Inspirational Speaker

I asked Captain Fitch some specific questions about Turbulence. Following is what I learned:

Jet With Kids:
Taking the Fear Out of Flying
WITH YOUR KIDS!

52

Turbulence is a disturbance or collision of air masses.

"To be scientific about it...it's a disturbance or in some cases a collision of air masses. It has almost a 3D capability. The difficulty with turbulence is that it can't be seen. It's an air mass and they classically can not be determined in directional terms; we don't know whether air is going up, down, left, right, forward, or aft. That's what makes it very very difficult from the pilot's perspective. And it is a disturbance; it's either a change in the flow of velocity, it's a change in the flow of direction, [or] it can be a combination of both." (Capt. Fitch, 40 years of experience as pilot)

Some form of this is common, and does occur on most every flight. There are many things that can cause turbulence. A few of the things that Capt. Denny Fitch, Sr. mentioned to cause turbulence are:

1) weather – thunderstorms, hurricanes in other areas, change of seasons

2) different jet streams colliding (like two cars hitting each other broadside)

3) different terrain such as mountains, causing different air flows over the ground

4) going through another airline's jet wake

5) change in velocity or direction of air flow or a combination of both

There are different ways that pilots are warned of the possibility of turbulence:

• Meteorologists combine circumstances they see developing with the weather along with historical data or behaviors, and can make a good predication of what may happen in certain conditions. This gives the pilot an opportunity to take a course of action to avoid heavy turbulence.

• Other pilots who have flown through the area recently also provide a valuable tool for predicting turbulence. However, as Capt. Fitch pointed out, we all know that weather can change rapidly.

> **Capt. Fitch states that the difficult thing about turbulence is that it is very hard to look ahead and see it by electronic or technical means. Clear air turbulence is most difficult to forecast and predict and not possible to detect because it is invisible.**

Severe Turbulence

What is unusual is to find severe turbulence...severe turbulence is something that is something you don't want to get into for any reason, whether you are strapped in or not. You simply don't want to get into severe turbulence so we do our very very best with all the tools we do have to avoid any possibility that we'll get ourselves in those areas. We will purposely change course and steer in directions that will burn more fuel, take more time, but it will avoid the harm that a severe turbulent event would cause. (Capt. Fitch, 40 years of experience as a pilot)

> **Even though everyone works together to warn of areas of turbulence, the reality is that it is always changing, can have varying degrees of severity and is invisible. Severe turbulence is very rare, but it does happen.**

The Australian Government Civil Aviation Safety Authority has an easy-to-read, informative website on turbulence. http://www.casa.gov.au/airsafe/trip/turbulen.htm

I have recently learned of the tragedy of the baby that was thrown up in the air and suffered <u>fatal</u> head injuries from hitting the ceiling during severe turbulence. On a separate occasion, there was a flight out of Japan that encountered such severe turbulence; a woman was killed when her neck was broken. The plane was so trashed that it had to be retired after that flight. Severe turbulence is very real and

Jet With Kids:
Taking the Fear Out of Flying
WITH YOUR KIDS!

54

for those who encounter it, very scary and can be extremely dangerous.

As Capt. Fitch states, *Severe turbulence is a very rare phenomenon. It does happen, it's not unheard of, but it's very unusual, and most of the time when it happens it comes out of nowhere because nobody expected it. It's usually short lived and it's very abrupt and severe. The airplanes typically can tolerate it from a physical point of view, but if anybody is not secured within their seats or seatbelts fastened it's a very high probability there's going to be injuries.* (Capt. Fitch, 40 years of experience as pilot)

Holding a lap child against forces such as turbulence or the horrible forces of a crash is just not a reality. When I asked Capt. Fitch his thoughts on the lap child policy, he stated this, *My own daughter will not travel without the seatbelt. All their children at all ages will either be seat belted in when they're in their seats, and if they were of infant age, they were definitely in a child seat and strapped in as well. I think she just inferred from all the experiences I've had in my career, 34 years of flying airplanes, that there were enough opportunities there to harm her children so she felt it was worth the economics, so to speak, to put forth the money to buy the seat, to have a child seat. Even if nothing happened there was at least peace of mind that there would be no harm because of the child's stature, how he/she was placed in the aircraft.* (Capt. Fitch, 40 years experience as pilot)

> **Living in denial does not protect your child.**
> **In the event of turbulence during a flight, your infant/toddler deserves the same protection provided to those passengers *over* the age of 24 months by FAA required seatbelt restraints. Most injuries caused by turbulence occur to those who are not properly restrained.**

There are also times that the seat belt sign and pilot announcement happen *after* the initial turbulence hits. Flight Attendant A tells her account of being knocked unconscious before she could notify the pilot about the turbulence:

"I got knocked out once (from turbulence in the) back . . . and I bent over just to call the captain to say, 'Hey, it's getting bumpy,' and that's the last thing I remember. It shook so bad, and because I was leaned over sideways, I hit the floor, and the next thing I know I opened my eyes and they are all going, 'Oh my gosh!' I mean that fast." (Flight Attendant A, 28 years experience)

 ## Seat Belt Around Both Adult and Child

Some parents think that it is okay to put their seat belt around both their child and themselves. This may seem like an acceptable option; however, the force of turbulence or a crash will throw your body weight (which multiplies with G force) against your child.

> **Your body weight will crush your child right there in your lap.**

I've seen women strap their infants in the same seat belt as them, and then I have to explain to them they can't do that because what if we were barreling down the runway ready to take off. We're going 100 miles per hour and we have to abort takeoff. We slam on the breaks. What happens to your weight? You go forward and your baby is locked in the seat belt, and you are crushing the baby. So that's why you have to be the seat belt and you have to be very conscious of it. (Renée, Retired Flight Attendant, 36 years experience)

There are some products available that claim to protect your child during turbulence. These products are not approved for use during takeoff and landing. These are the most dangerous times and your child is only safe in an approved car seat. Also, as many parents have told me, most airlines will not allow your child to wear these products since it is confusing as to when they are allowed to be worn according to airline policy.

What I wanted as a parent was information that would allow me to make an informed decision. What I heard instead were reservation agents repeatedly telling me that I should not purchase a seat for my infant (under two) since he could fly for FREE! As a new mother facing a flight with a newborn baby, there are many other things that consume energy and time while planning for a trip. And many parents are feeling the crunch of a tighter budget; maybe the mom is staying home or taking time off for maternity leave.

The bills of all the necessary baby items cut into the amount in the vacation fund and so when someone from the airline is *discouraging* about buying a seat, what would make a mother say- 'No really, I would LIKE to pay the $300 or whatever amount'? The only thing that I can think of is that mother knowing that **her baby is only safe being restrained in a child safety seat**. Knowing that if turbulence did happen, it would be *her* life that was forever affected by an injury – maybe even a fatal injury to her sweet precious baby. Do not leave the fate of your child's safety to someone that is not providing all of the facts.

> **Realize that many times in life, you are the only person that your children can depend on to be their advocate. Don't let them down at a time when they are most defenseless.**

Take responsibility... purchase a seat...buckle them in... and feel good about your child being offered the same protection that you are receiving. And don't be afraid to send an email to the FAA, voicing your concern about how they are keeping aviation safe... only for those passengers older than 24 months!

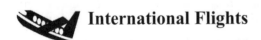 **International Flights**

> **All passengers regardless of age must have a ticket and a passport for international flights. (A ticket does not mean a seat has been purchased.)**

Yes, even those booked as lap children and infants are required to purchase a ticket on international flights. Lap children are charged taxes and surcharges, such as a fuel surcharge. These charges added up to more than $200 on our flight to Europe. And yet, my son was still considered a lap child and without a seat.

 ## Ticket Pricing—Child Discount

Child fares are discounted, but sometimes it is only off of the adult full fare, which can be more expensive than the promo adult fare. Therefore, it may be cheaper to actually buy the adult fare for the child rather than the "discounted" child fare. However, it is always a good idea to ask about the discounted rate and compare.

 ## The 23-Month-and-Holding Child

Some parents think that it might work to pretend their child is still under two years old to save money. They may even get away with it for the first leg or two of the flight (on domestic flights, where a passport isn't required). However, when a ticket agent 2,000 miles from home demands to see a birth certificate, that idea to save money will backfire as you may then be charged a much higher rate than if you had purchased the ticket in advance. Sometimes to prove the point, you will be charged a one-way full fare (last-minute rate).

> *If they question it, it's your responsibility to prove the age of the baby. If they think the baby is over 2, and you don't have a ticket, they will make you buy one . . . it's usually a last-minute one-way full fare ticket . . . domestically they run from $800–$1,200. Internationally they run $1,200–$1,800.* (Reservations Agent, 7 years experience)

Jet With Kids:
Taking the Fear Out of Flying
WITH YOUR KIDS!

58

 ## Advantage of Purchasing a Seat

I have found that purchasing a seat for your infant is a great advantage. As every parent knows, if you give your child their own space, they are happier and not as likely to squirm. The car seat is something familiar to children, and they will feel as though they are in the car. It is wonderful to know that they are secure if there is turbulence. A car seat also provides a great place for them to sleep.

I have found that when I'm holding my son on my lap, no matter where we are, he tends to be more restless and wants to get down. Yet, when he is buckled into his car seat on the airplane, he tends to stay put and sleeps much better.

> **The car seat is a familiar place where he is normally buckled in and not allowed to be unbuckled.**

Just like in the car, on a plane it is often necessary to distract a child to keep him happy. Treat safety procedures on the plane the same as you would in a car.

I realize that there are people who disagree with my views on lap child policies. Until the FAA makes a seat mandatory, many parents will continue to save money, ignore or deny the risk, and allow their child to fly as a lap child. My hope is that if I can provide this information, other parents like me, who blindly trusted the FAA, will be completely informed before making their decision.

> **Yes, the odds are in your favor of nothing happening.**
> **Are you willing to risk your child's life and chance it?**
> **I would never want you to feel the devastation**
> **and loss that Evan's parents feel.**

Chapter 7

Car Seat Considerations

 Counting on the Empty Seat

In the past, it was possible to hope for an empty seat next to you, that you could put your car seat in and avoid the cost of a ticket for your child under 2. However, today flights are full, and as I personally found out (before I wrote this and realized the danger of the lap child), policies are changing and gate agents will enforce them. A major airline has recently created a policy that bans car seats from being allowed in a seat unless you purchased the seat. Because of this policy, I was not allowed to put my son's car seat in the empty seat next to me since I did not purchase a ticket for him. So my young son sat on my lap during takeoff and landing and sat unbuckled in the empty seat for the rest of the flight.

**A lot of online sources state that parents should bring the car seat along, and if the seat is open- it is yours to use. This is not always true and can be stressful for parents who rely on this!*

> **If you do not purchase a seat, the empty one next to you will not necessarily be available for you to use.**
> **You may not even be allowed to take your car seat onboard without purchasing a seat for your child.**

 Is Your Car Seat Approved for Flight?

All airlines recommend that you purchase a seat and have an FAA approved car seat for your child. Please take note that the car

Jet With Kids:
Taking the Fear Out of Flying
WITH YOUR KIDS!

60

seat MUST be FAA approved. Gate Agent B, (28 years airline experience), informed me that gate agents are suppose to check for this sticker and apply a tag to show that it has been approved. Flight attendants as well check for the sticker. Since sometimes car seats are passed down through the years, make sure that the sticker has not worn off, since they will not allow it for use on the aircraft.

> **FAA approved means it must say, "this child restraint system conforms to all applicable Federal Motor Vehicle Safety Standards" and "This Restraint is Certified for Use in Motor Vehicles and Aircraft"**

 ## Forward- or Rear-Facing Seat

> **The FAA recommends**
> - **a rear-facing Child Restraint Seat (CRS) be used for children under 20 pounds; (some foreign airlines do not allow this)**
> - **a forward-facing CRS be used for children 20–40 pounds; and**
> - **an airline seat belt be used for children weighing more than 40 pounds.**

http://www.faa.gov/passengers/fly_children/crs/

Make sure your car seat is FAA approved and follow the weight regulations.
http://www.babycenter.com/expert/baby/babytravel/1348015.html

 ## Staying Comfortable in the Seat

Following are some great travel products from Traveling With Kids to keep your child comfortable in his car seat.

Feet Seat or Foot'z Rest
(http://www.JetWithKidsClub.com/seat) — Think about how uncomfortable it is to sit in a chair with your legs dangling. Keep your children comfortable by using these products as a support for their feet.

Snack & Play Travel Tray
(**http://www.JetWithKidsClub.com/transport**) — The aircraft tray does not fit over the car seat. This product allows the child to have a clean surface to play on and eat on. It can be placed over the car seat through the airport, in a car, and on a plane.

> *My son uses this tray over his car seat in the plane. He spent hours playing with his cars lined up on the tray. It was also a clean surface for his food. It has a flexible surface and can be used in the car or in the airport.*
> *(Anya's review)*

Transporting the Car Seat

There are more and more products that you can buy now that help you to carry the car seat through the airport.

1) Transporting car seats—two options:
One that I absolutely love is called
   *Go-Go Kidz Travelmate Car Seat Trolley
(**http://www.JetWithKidsClub.com/transport**) is the sturdier option that can be wheeled right down the aisle of the plane to your airplane seat (push handle of trolley down).

> *The Go-Go Kidz has taken the work out of transporting the car seat through the airport. Many people stop us in the airport to ask where we purchased this product. It actually can be wheeled right to your seat! The first flight I used it on, I applied it to our Britax Marathon car seat. This seat was too wide to roll down the aisle of the plane. I later found out that if you want to use the trolley with a Britax car seat you should use the Britax Roundabout, as that is narrow enough to fit down most aisles.*
> *(Anya's review)*

*Traveling Toddler
(**http://www.JetWithKidsClub.com/transport**) is a strap that works with any latch/tether car seat. It is an inexpensive way to strap the car seat (child and all) onto your suitcase and wheel them through the airport. You might need to take this apart on the jet way before getting on the aircraft, but it provides a great way to haul your car seat through the airport.

 I first tried out the traveling toddler strap on our trip to London and Vienna, and was very happy with it! The car seat was tightly secured to the rolling suitcase using the Latch system. We had to remove it for security and then again when boarding the plane, but it was wonderful wheeling it onto the Underground Tube in London, through Heathrow airport and on our way to Vienna over the cobblestone streets of Vienna, and back through Heathrow on the layover going home. It is an economical way to alleviate the hassle of physically carrying the car seat. (Anya's Review)

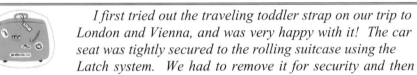 **Booster Seats**

The FAA does not allow booster seats and states that they should be checked as baggage to your destination. See below for a brand new option for keeping your child (weight 22-44 lbs.) safe:

 CARES Harness

It was on my latest flight to Hawaii, as I was crouched over the seat wrestling with my son's car seat, sweat running down my back, that I first heard of Louise Stoll. A friendly flight attendant was empathizing with me as I struggled to get my son's bulky car seat installed in the airplane seat.

I sat intrigued, listening as the flight attendant told me about the new product that had just a few days before been announced as being FAA certified. After watching The Today Show that morning before our flight, she was able to inform me of all that she knew of this new harness option designed to replace the bulky car seat on planes.

I was so excited and could hardly wait to arrive in Kona so that I could check it out. Sure enough, I had multiple emails and voice mails from my travel expert friends telling me that I had to find out what this product was about.

An answer to my prayers had arrived! After putting my name on the preorder list, I contacted Louise Stoll, the grandmother of 8 who had so ingeniously invented this lifesaving product.

We had a long, informative, friendly conversation, and today I am excited to share this news with other traveling parents. I love products that were designed by someone who was fed up with the old system. Louise realized there had to be an easier way for parents to travel with their children after watching her pregnant daughter carry a bulky car seat, a toddler and a diaper bag off of a plane.

She proceeded to design the new safety harness, called CARES. This harness is designed for children between the weight of 22 lbs and 44 lbs, ages 1-4, and who are seated in their own seat. It is a shoulder harness that is used with the lap belt of the airplane seat. This can be used on any seat of any plane, except for exit rows.

> **The great thing about this harness is that it only weighs 1 pound and is small enough to fit in your pocket!**

A long tedious process of attaining FAA approval was finally finished in August 2006. AmSafe Aviation, the same company that provides safety harnesses for pilots and flight attendants, manufactures the harness.

The FAA has added this harness to the recommended list of child safety restraints, and feature a photo of the harness in use on their website. The FAA has approved CARES to be furnished and

Jet With Kids:
Taking the Fear Out of Flying
WITH YOUR KIDS!

64

used by parents on all commercial and private flights in the US. At this time, airlines are not providing this product for their passengers. http://www.faa.gov/passengers/fly_children/crs/

Louise's product has caught national media attention. Check out these informative sites for more information:

The Today Show Segment (The video segment plays after the commercial is finished – be patient!) http://video.msn.com/v/us/msnbc.htm?g=40b925b2-dba9-4dbd-b433-4d398f3234a8&f=00&fg=email

National Public Radio (NPR) http://marketplace.publicradio.org/shows/2006/09/06/PM200609067.html

Now if you want, you can check your car seat as checked luggage or gate check it (if you want to use Go-Go Kidz Travelmate Car Seat Trolley **(http://www.JetWithKidsClub.com/transport)** and your car seat as a stroller through the airport).

Since this is a brand new product, there are sure to be some airline employees who have not yet been educated about this new FAA approved device. You are able to print out the brochure from the FAA's website listed above. Louise informed me that the harness will come with information specifically printed for this purpose as well.

> **Be patient, as it often takes time for new policies to reach the whole industry. However, know that since the CARES harness is FAA certified for use in take off, landing, and turbulence (the most dangerous times of flight), NOBODY can prevent you from using this onboard a US flight.**

As of November 2006, CARES is not approved on foreign carriers, as they are not governed by the FAA.

To order a CARES harness:
http://www.JetWithKidsClub.com/seat

Note: For babies under 22 lbs., you must still bring the infant car seat on board.

 I first practiced using the CARES harness on a chair in my living room as I watched the DVD instructional video. It was very easy to use, and incredibly light (only weighs 1 lb.)!

From the packaging to the instructional card (same design as safety cards on commercial aircraft), and the convenient pouch to carry the harness, everything about the CARES harness is professionally done.

The middle seat was empty and this is where I first used the CARES harness. The flight attendant had heard of the device and allowed its use on board. My son was happy to sit on the big seat like me, and be able to use his own tray table. The harness fit easily over the back of the seat and since he is familiar with a 5-point harness on his car seat, it was a quick process to install the harness.

Wow, I was amazed at how quick and easy it was to install! No more pre-boarding necessary and no more stressful car seat installations with pinched fingers for me! And the best part is, no big bulky car seat to lug around!

Since my son is a frequent flier, using the harness was a change for him. I recommend practicing with the harness at home so installation is familiar to parents as well as children. And be patient with airline personnel as this is a new product. Carry along the instructional card (although the instructions are also on the harness), as well as the FAA regulations (can be found at http://www.JetWithKidsClub.com/resources), which demonstrate that the CARES harness is approved for take off, landing, and use in flight on airlines governed by the FAA.

The price is worth it for anyone traveling with children, since the convenience and ease of use will save you time, energy and the hassle of carrying a car seat through the airport! (Anya's Review)

Jet With Kids:
Taking the Fear Out of Flying
WITH YOUR KIDS!

66

Chapter 8

Important Documentation Requirements

> **It is your responsibility to make sure that you have all required documentation before flying. The airlines are not responsible for educating you about what documentation is needed. I've found they may even refer you to immigration when you inquire about proper documentation on the phone.**

 ## Passport Guidelines: United States

The U.S. Department of State website provides information for obtaining a passport and answers questions about international travel: http://travel.state.gov/

Who needs a passport?

> **Every passenger traveling to a foreign country, whether an infant, child, or adult, is required to have his or her own passport.**

Some border countries do not require passports yet, but soon this will change as well.
As of January 23, 2007:
http://travel.state.gov/travel/cbpmc/cbpmc_2223.html
http://travel.state.gov/passport/passport_1738.html

The following link shows foreign entry requirements. You are able to select the country of interest, and it tells you which documentation is needed to enter that country.
http://travel.state.gov/travel/tips/brochures/brochures_1229.html

General information for obtaining a U.S. Passport:

http://travel.state.gov/passport/fri/pubs/pubs_854.html

Where can I obtain a certified birth certificate?

The hospital certificate is not certified. This can be confusing. Visit the Center for Disease Control link and select the state where the birth occurred to get mailing information for requesting a certified birth certificate if you do not have one already.

http://www.cdc.gov/nchs/howto/w2w/w2welcom.htm

What are the passport requirements for minors?

Passport Requirements for Minors
1. Completed application
2. Proof of citizenship
3. Proof of child's relationship to parent/guardian
4. Both parents' photo identification
5. Both parents must be present or provide a notarized consent from the missing parent
6. 2 passport photos
7. Fee
8. Social Security Number

http://www.travel.state.gov/passport/get/minors/minors_834.html

Where can I get a passport?

United States post offices accept passport applications. Enter your zip code at the following link to get a list of passport facilities near you: http://iafdb.travel.state.gov/

Jet With Kids:
Taking the Fear Out of Flying
WITH YOUR KIDS!

68

How long does it take to get a passport?

Allow a minimum of at least 6 weeks to receive your passport. However there are expediting services that can process your application quicker, for an increased fee.
http://www.travel.state.gov/passport/get/processing/processing_1740.html

Although with the new requirement—see below (everyone will need passports to go to Canada, Mexico, and the Caribbean)—longer processing times are likely.

How long does a passport last before it expires?

Age 16 and older—valid for 10 years
Age 15 and under—valid for 5 years

http://travel.state.gov/passport/fri/faq/faq_1741.html#valid

This site recommends that you renew 9 months before expiration. So if you are planning an international trip next year, why not get the process started now and have one less thing to worry about?

What are the passport fees?

For 16 years and older: $97.00
For 15 years and younger: $82.00

Since these fees may change, it is best to check with the U.S. Department of State website for the most up-to-date fees.

http://www.travel.state.gov/passport/get/fees/fees_837.html

Budget for this in advance since a family of five can add up fast (especially if you need to expedite delivery time).
Kathryn, a travel agent with 35 years of experience, advises parents to split this cost over several months, by taking one child at a time to get this done.

Starting December 31ˢᵗ of this year, they're all going to need passports. I am telling people to take one kid in September, and one kid in October, and one kid in November so they're not all at one $500 check for a family of five. Just break it up. That's your little day, you go pick them up after school, you go to the post office, [and] get it done. (Kathryn Sudeikis, CTC- Travel Agent, 35 years experience)

If I have a passport, does my child need one, too?

Yes, all children must have their own passport.
http://www.travel.state.gov/passport/get/minors/minors_834.html

What are the new passport requirements?

As of January 23, 2007, "all air and sea travel to and from Canada, Mexico, Central and South America, the Caribbean, and Bermuda" will require a passport.

As of January 1, 2008, this requirement will be applied to land travel as well.
http://travel.state.gov/travel/cbpmc/cbpmc_2223.html

 **Notarized Letter**

When you are traveling internationally with your children, and their other parent is not with you, a notarized letter giving you permission to travel with the children is required.

> *The notarized letter is essentially needed for any travel outside of the United States . . . and the idea is to protect the child from being kidnapped by a parent or guardian. . . . The letter is [needed] whenever you are traveling with a child that is not your own child or*

Jet With Kids:
Taking the Fear Out of Flying
WITH YOUR KIDS!

70

both parents are not traveling with the child. (Kathryn Sudeikis, CTC -Travel Agent, 35 years experience)

Examples include meeting your spouse on a business trip, taking a nephew along to play with your son, or taking a child's friend along with your family. A notarized letter may also be required when you are traveling with your child internationally as a single parent. Check with the consular information:
http://travel.state.gov/travel/warnings_consular.html

If one parent is deceased, a death certificate is required. I found a sample consent letter at Cruise Diva's website:
http://cruisediva.com/permission_ltr.htm

Chapter 9

The Flight Process: Booking

As you're going through the travel process, please treat those you come into contact with, with respect. Be polite and do not think being forceful, loud, or obnoxious will get you your desired results. This will have the opposite effect most of the time. Think about how this flight is affecting your child.

> **It is easy to think only about how you will get through the journey as a parent, but remember that for your child everything is new and can be scary or exciting. Take time to explain what is happening.**

It can be frustrating when dealing with the airlines and getting conflicting information for your flight plans. I was amazed at the results of a little experiment I did. I asked five people to call various airlines, both domestic and foreign. I then gave them each the same list of questions to ask about booking flights for an unaccompanied minor as well as about flying with children.

We were astonished to hear the wide range of answers that we were given from different reservation agents working for the same airline. For some questions, we heard the exact opposite answers, and many times the answers were vague. No wonder flying can be frustrating! You may also find that the airline reservation agent is not the friendliest or easiest person to work with. Please realize that for the most part they are providing you with what they believe to be the correct answer. The airline industry as a whole has gone through major changes and continues to be a difficult environment to work in.

Jet With Kids:
Taking the Fear Out of Flying
WITH YOUR KIDS!

72

Many of these hard-working airline employees are now faced with huge pay cuts, downsizing, and insecurity about their future, and more work is often expected of them for less pay.

I also did not realize until I started interviewing those in the airline industry that some reservation agents are timed, and their focus is to get your credit card number in the system so they have something to show for the call. This might explain the rudeness we encountered when we asked questions and they had to look up the answers. Once again, I am sure that this is not by choice, and they have to think about keeping their job.

If you call and get an unfriendly or rude employee, even though you face holding time again, call back. Get the speaker phone out, call when the kids are asleep, and work on other things while you wait. It can make a huge difference in how much the employee is willing to work with you. I have called back and been booked on flights that I had been told were unavailable. I've also been assigned seats together with my traveling companions when previously I was told there were none. The second agent I talked to was willing to be creative.

I have also found this to be true when trying to book frequent flier tickets using miles. Sometimes it takes a creative, patient agent to help you find an available flight. I have found that it is worth it to call back and talk to a friendlier agent when my questions are harshly and impatiently answered. I also think that it does not hurt to kindly and gently mention to the agent that they sound like they are stressed and you understand that they may have had a bad day and that you will call back for a friendlier agent. I have had some agents then realize that they were being rude and apologize and then prove to be extremely helpful!

Like in any job where you work with people all day, it can be difficult to deal with the public. You may be friendly, but realize that the public in general is stressed and can be demanding. Especially if a customer has had a previous bad experience, it is usually the innocent employee that bears the brunt of this frustration.

So throughout your flight experience, maintain your patience and try to deal with those who are willing to help you. I have realized more than ever after writing this, that many of these employees are going through extremely stressful times with their jobs. And yes, since time is money, many times it is worth it to call your travel agent and let them take care of your travel needs!

> **Keep in mind that each airline is different, and as each reservations agent may give you a slightly different answer, always confirm your flight information when checking in for your flight.**

 ## It's All in the Ratio!

When we went to Europe, my mom went with us. When you need to go to the restroom, you can. We took turns [walking around with our child]. The ratio with more adults or more help really makes a big difference. (Gilly, Traveling Mom, 6 years experience)

Traveling as parents, the vacation is spent exactly as that—parents. One person tends to take care of the travel documents, checking in and staying organized, while the other parent takes care of the child and all of his needs.

When traveling, it is sometimes advisable to look into other options than the conventional two-parent system. How about taking grandma along or a good friend? Even traveling with another family with children around the same age could prove to be more enjoyable in many instances.

We elected to take a good friend of ours along to Europe. We rotated childcare, so each of us was able to have time to enjoy the scenery as an adult.

> **We found that the ratio of adults to children can directly correspond to the level of enjoyment of our trip.**

Jet With Kids:
Taking the Fear Out of Flying
WITH YOUR KIDS!

74

The flights were so much more enjoyable as there were now three people to entertain my son. And especially when you are in a foreign place, it is nice to have an extra person to navigate while one adult focuses on childcare and the other is backup or handles the luggage or language translation.

Even if you are traveling domestically, if this is your only time away from work to recharge your batteries, do yourselves and your children a favor by bringing along the baby-sitter or someone you can trust. Remember that this is your vacation; use judgment in deciding whom you will ask to come along. It is so important as parents to remember that your significant other is more than just a mother or father, and by increasing the ratio, your stress level may decrease enough to see that!

As Carole, a commercial pilot and traveling mom of triplets says, *"we still take a helper . . . because with three 4-year-olds . . . we are just outnumbered and it's no fun at all if we don't have that [help]. It's just nicer to have that one-on-one time."*

 The Solo Parent Traveler

I realize it is not always possible to have more than one adult traveling together. This does not mean flying as a solo parent cannot be done successfully! As I researched the solo/single parent traveler, one name consistently came up. Brenda Elwell is an expert on traveling with children—and doing so as a single parent. She has been to 67 countries, half of those with her children! She has been an inspiration and a strong advocate for parents traveling with children. She states that children who have traveled are more comfortable with cultural differences.

They're much more worldly in their outlook. They're much more tolerant of physical as well as cultural differences. I see it in my own kids, and they would have learned that to a degree from me just telling them or teaching them as a parent, but to experience it for themselves in that culture was enlightening for them. (Brenda Elwell, Single Parent Travel Expert, 40 years experience)

She has written a book that is good for everyone with children to read. Her tips are tried and true, and her stories are entertaining. She was kind enough to spend some time with me in a phone conversation to talk about how to visit the world with children. My original intent in contacting her was to get tips on the single/solo parent traveler, and instead I came away with wonderful tips and a respect for her as a family travel advocate.

Her book is filled with useful tips for all nontraditional families; yet I, as part of a traditional two-parent family, benefited greatly from her advice. I think any trip where the children are properly prepared and involved and kept safe and informed is going to be a good trip for any type of family.

Even in a traditional family, there are times in the life of a child when one parent will travel alone with him to visit the other on business or to visit one side of the family. Beth McGregor, a traveling mom, states that sometimes it was easier for her traveling as the solo parent than as part of a team of two, since there was only one person in charge.

> **Brenda Elwell explains that the one common thing she noted between single moms and dads who enjoy travel with their children is that they are devoted to the child having a good time.**

The trip was really not so much geared toward the child, but the parent was devoted to seeing that the child had a good time. They were focused on that, not to the extent that they didn't have a good time as well, but it was very important to them that the child have a good time, because they knew that if the child had a good time, they would have a good time. They wanted them both to enjoy it. (Brenda Elwell, Single Parent Travel Expert, 40 years experience)

Jet With Kids:
Taking the Fear Out of Flying
WITH YOUR KIDS!

76

To purchase Brenda's book:
The Single Parent Travel Handbook:
http://www.JetWithKidsClub.com/tools

 Frequent Flier Miles

I am surprised to find out that many people fly without a frequent flier number. Even newborn babies can have a frequent flier number, and as long as they are sitting in a purchased seat with a qualifying fare, they will earn miles (check with your airline for their rules and regulations).

**A frequent flier number is free to obtain
(you must call the airline or your travel agent and request a number,
or sign up online), and the miles usually do not expire.**

These miles can be used for upgrades on certain fares and for free tickets. I tend to save mine for unexpected, last-minute flights, when I can save the most money!

However, I will caution you that during peak travel times (summer months and spring break or holidays), it is virtually impossible to use frequent flier miles to obtain a free flight. There is a very limited amount of free tickets available, and they are usually gone as soon as they become available. Some airlines have recently made changes to their frequent flier programs. Check with your airline to verify.

Some of the low-cost airlines allow you to have any open seat on that flight using your frequent flier miles or points. Please check well in advance with your airline of choice.

Amanda Gengler, a staff reporter for *Money Magazine,* wrote an article for CNN commenting on how easy it has become to obtain

frequent flier miles and how difficult it can be to actually redeem them.
http://money.cnn.com/magazines/moneymag/moneymag_archive/200
6/08/01/8382161/index.htm

Even though they can be difficult to redeem at times, frequent flier miles are still a great savings tool for frequent travelers. These miles are also available to be used on some fares as an upgrade to fly first class. You are usually able to book someone else a ticket using your miles as long as you do the booking.

You must either enter your frequent flier number in your reservation when booking online or provide it for the travel agent, reservation agent, or gate agent. It is your responsibility to remember this since the airline agents usually do not ask.

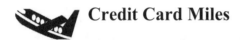 ## Credit Card Miles

Another way to increase your miles in your frequent flier account is to use a credit card to earn miles.

> My husband and I figured out long ago that since we were going to spend money on groceries, gas, and household goods, we might as well get at least one or two miles per dollar that we could use toward our travels.

This adds up quickly and can make it easier to obtain a free flight or upgrade. I recommend that you pay off your credit card balance every month to avoid paying interest and losing any financial gain!

Here is a site that lists the credit cards and airline and hotel partners that let you earn free miles:
http://www.indexcreditcards.com/travel_airlinecreditcards.html

 ## Code Share Flights

As more and more airlines are becoming partners, it is important to note which airline your flight will be **operated** by. This can be difficult to find since it is sometimes in small writing.

> **You will want to abide by the operating airline's policies and check in for your flight at the operating airline's counter.**

28 year airline veteran, Gate Agent B, states that it can be a hassle to wait in line only to find out you are in the wrong terminal and now face missing your flight. Even if you book your flight through carrier A, if carrier B operates it, you will need to check in with carrier B for the flight.

This is also true for certain seat assignments or special requests. If you're booking the reservations yourself, always call the operating airline to confirm your reservation and request. If you use a travel agent, they will handle this for you; however, confirm with them which airline you are actually flying on for each leg of your trip.

 ## Seat Assignments

At http://www.seatguru.com you can find all of the details about the aircraft you'll fly on, including the seat width, legroom, and so forth. This site also contains contact information for the airlines.

I am always amazed when the flight is full or even overbooked, and the frazzled parent is begging the gate agent to arrange for her family to have seats together.

> **Do not assume that since you are a family you will be seated together! You must make your seat assignment in advance for that to happen.**

Gate Agent B, (28 years airline experience) stated, *"I know that a 2-year-old shouldn't be sitting alone, but when you arrive without seat assignments 5 minutes before the door closes, it makes it extremely difficult to get the family together!"* The reality is that your family may be seated all throughout the plane.

I understand that there are times when flights are booked at the last minute, plans are changed, or the option of selecting seats is not given when booking due to a full flight.

There are only a certain number of seats that reservation and travel agents are able to book. The rest are blocked out for airport assignment on the day of departure or for online check-in 24 hours prior to the flight. However, unless you are booking at the last minute, it is usually possible for you to get something reserved, and seat selection can make a *huge* difference in your flight.

> **It is always advisable to book yourself a seat assignment in advance, even if you cannot get seats together.**

(Please note that some low-cost airlines do not have advance seat assignment, so it pays to check in early—24 hours in advance online or as early as possible at the airport to get a boarding "group," which designates who gets to board first. Although some of these airlines do allow parents with children under the age of 4, to pre-board.)

1.   <u>Try to reserve window and aisle seats, as these are good bartering tools.</u> (Nobody wants to sit in a middle seat!) If you have something to work with, you are more likely to get cooperation and someone to trade seats with you onboard so that your family can be together. (I also like to book the window and aisle seat in hopes that the flight is not full and the middle seat will remain empty. It is always worth a try!)

2.   <u>Don't assume that since you are flying as a family, people should give up their reserved seats for you.</u> It is possible that they reserved months in advance and planned their seat assignment for a specific

Jet With Kids:
Taking the Fear Out of Flying
WITH YOUR KIDS!

80

reason. **Many people are kind and respond much better to a smile, eye contact, and a genuine request instead of a demand.**

> **Please note that on some airlines, there is a new option for people to purchase "preferred" seats the day of departure for around $15. Don't be offended if others do not want to move, since they have a right to their seat.**

3.   I have found that sometimes it is nice to purposely book my husband and I *separately* so that my son has a different person to interact with once in a while and we can switch spots when one of us gets tired. If you are traveling with more than one adult, I have found it advantageous at times to sit with one adult next to your child and one adult in front of your child. Kicking a stranger's seat is not an issue, and games of peek-a-boo or surprise are free entertainment. Your family will be together the whole vacation; it might be nice to meet some new people on the flight!

4.   Seats in the Exit row are not an option when traveling with children. The airlines do not allow children under the age of 15 to sit in an exit row in case of an emergency. This extra legroom also will be much appreciated by the off-duty pilot who has a big flight ahead (maybe even on your next flight!), or the tall person that physically cannot fit into the regular seats comfortably.

There is also a rule that prevents anyone traveling with children from sitting in the exit row. This means that Dad is not allowed to sit in the exit row, since he is part of a family. In the case of an emergency, he will have an obligation to the other passengers as well as to his family, who are not seated next to him. This could be a distraction for him and prevent him from effectively completing the duties of those seated in the exit row. This policy is for the safety of *everyone* traveling.

Anyone who has other responsibilities, such as animals or traveling with children seated elsewhere who are younger than 15, [are not allowed to sit in the exit row]. (Flight Attendant A, 28 years experience)

5. <u>Bulkhead seats are reserved for airport check-in</u>. Many times there is a big demand for the bulkhead seats. One nice feature is that there is no row in front of you for your child to kick! Although sometimes the bassinet is an option for infants on international flights (not very safe in case of turbulence), there are many downsides to having a seat in this row when traveling with children. It is true that there is typically more legroom here. However, there is, as travel agent Kathryn Sudeikis states, the "Bulkhead Myth":

a. This added legroom gives a child the feeling of open space and the illusion that they can roam around. As Kathryn points out, if you take the middle seat of another row and your child is in the window seat next to you, this area creates a "box" for your child to play in. They can play with the window shade, on the tray table, look out the window, and generally feel more secure since it is somewhat of a private area.

b. All of your belongings are required to be stowed in the overhead compartment during takeoff and landing. There normally isn't a storage pocket in front of you and you cannot put anything below your seat. Prepare for this as you can be stuck on the runway for a long time and don't want to be empty-handed and trying to entertain or care for a young one. Take out a small book, rattle, or something that you can hold to entertain your child. Also remember to have something for them to eat or drink or a pacifier for takeoff and landing.

c. The tray tables are not in front of you; they are located in the armrests and they can easily pinch little fingers. This also means that the armrests do not go up and therefore, your movement is restricted.

d. The video screens can sometimes be more difficult to see from this position, as they are directly in front of and above your row.

Jet With Kids:
Taking the Fear Out of Flying
WITH YOUR KIDS!

82

e.   The bulkhead row tends to be a noisier area during the flight since that is where the line ends up forming for the restrooms located nearby. This can be a frustration if your little one just fell asleep.

6.   Bassinets are available only on international flights and on a first come, first served basis. **They are not to be used during takeoff, landing, or severe turbulence**. Therefore, I believe it is not a safe option since your child is held in the bassinet only by a Velcro closure on the flap.

7.   It is preferred by flight attendants and those concerned with safety, that car seats are only allowed in the window seat, although they are allowed in the middle section of the bigger planes. This is to prevent someone from being trapped by a car seat and not able to get out in case of an emergency.

Car seats also are not allowed in the row ahead of or behind the exit row in case more room is needed in an emergency. You need to take responsibility for this for your safety and that of other passengers.

> **The airlines will not necessarily ask if you are bringing a car seat, nor will they book only a window seat for your child and his car seat. It is up to you to ask for one.**

Also, it is best for car seats and children not to be in the aisle seat since they can be injured very easily by people or beverage carts going up the aisle.

8.   I like to have seats toward the back of the plane.
a.   **Pros:** You're likely to be near other families. If you have a crying toddler, the whole plane is not watching you try to entertain him! And, you are closer to the galley if you need to walk around a bit.

b. **Cons:** You are closer to the restrooms (but also all the smells and lines that come with being near them). The fact that there are more families can be a good distraction to your child or a bad one. You will feel the turbulence more in the back. I've been told that for a more stable feel, a seat over the wing is a good place to sit. Realize that your view out the window will be restricted.

Even though you may have made your seat selection months in advance, don't blindly trust the computers. Verify the seat assignment when you check in for your flight.

From my personal experience, I can tell you that change of aircraft or a computer glitch can double book seats or change the assignment. It is better to find this out ahead of time rather than when the plane is full of people and you and your child are facing other people in your seat.

 ## Parent in First Class and Child in Coach

A couple of airline employees I interviewed mentioned that it is not uncommon for parents to book themselves in first class and their children in coach. When you bring a child on the aircraft, you are still the responsible party. Do not book yourself in first class and assume that your children can sit in coach *unsupervised*.

Flight attendants are not baby-sitters, and neither are the passengers seated around your children.

This is not really the time to enjoy luxury while your job as a parent is handed over to other adults behind the curtain. Think about the implications if there was an emergency. Your children would need your care, and you may not be able to communicate with them if you are sitting in a separate section of the aircraft.

 ## Connection Times

Keep in mind that connecting through an airport with a child can take much longer than originally planned. Try to keep the day as calm as possible by booking flights that have long layovers (connection times). Running through the airport with a toddler in tow is not good for anyone and is bound to lead to tears from toddler, parent, or both!

> **Do not delay going to your gate, even if you do have a long layover. It is best to find bathrooms and restaurants *after* you have found your gate since it may be farther away than you had planned.**

I think that if you realize that the flight and travel to your destination are *part* of your vacation, it can make the whole process less stressful. Book connections that will allow you time to change diapers in a more spacious and sanitary environment than what is available on the airplane, change child's clothes if necessary (putting pajamas on for a night flight can help), and have some down time before boarding the next flight. Slow the process down and realize that many airports are like a small city. Those that work there will tell you that same thing.

Airports have a fire department, police department, and restaurants; some have salons and stores. This is a wonderful environment to people watch and get a glimpse of the world in a nutshell.

> **I am entranced by the life of the airport,**
> **and I think that many people miss some great entertainment by rushing through. Children soak up new sites and sounds and are much more likely to enjoy the process if you take time to enjoy it yourself!**

My son is only 2 years old, but I can tell he picks up on my anxiety in a stressful situation. Children take cues from those they trust. Is it really going to make a big difference in your trip if you risk making the quick connection just to arrive 2 hours earlier? Or will you and your family be exhausted from the stress and worry over needing to connect gates at opposite ends of the terminal?

Give yourself some time to make that connection. I recommend *at least* one and a half hours with a child. And with any extra time, look around and soak up the spirit of the world connecting and the miraculous environment surrounding you.

 ## Travel Insurance

Travel insurance protects your travel investment against cancellation or interruption. Ask questions and read the insurance policy carefully to know what your policy will cover. This is an absolute must when traveling with children. It is a wonderful protection of your investment of time and money and is most important if you have reserved a package or anything more than just a flight.

> **It is best to purchase insurance at the time you make your travel plans, since many plans have time limits on when they are available to purchase.**

There are some online companies that offer travel insurance and have comparison charts to compare different policies, allowing you to choose the best plan for your needs. I have used Insure My Trip in the past and have been happy with their response. My mom had a lost bag for 24 hours, and she was able to go to the store and buy needed items. They reimbursed her for her cost—I believe up to $150. I had actually encouraged her to buy it for the medical insurance portion, since she did not have coverage in a foreign country.

For a FREE Quote, Click on the Insure My Trip image at

http://www.JetWithKidsClub.com/links

Jet With Kids:
Taking the Fear Out of Flying
WITH YOUR KIDS!

86

 Tips for International Flights

1. Allow extra time for connections taking into consideration time to go through customs and the need to take care of tired children. Carole, a commercial pilot and traveling mom of triplets, summarizes her experience of traveling with tired children and having to clear customs in a short time frame:

> *My children were tired, the lines were long, the walk to customs and the gate was long, and when we arrived at the gate, the airplane door was closed. The airline personnel opened the door and let us in, but it was a stressful situation for all involved. Allow extra time for clearing customs.* (Carole, Commercial Pilot and Traveling Mom of triplets)

This is a checklist from the U.S. government, regarding customs:
http://www.customs.ustreas.gov/xp/cgov/travel/vacation/kbyg/travelers_checklist.xml

2. As soon as you can, ask your physician or a travel clinic what shots (if any) are required for your trip. Some things, such as typhoid shots need to be ordered ahead of time or spaced out.

> *Don't wait a week before you leave to find out if you need any shots. You should plan about three months before hand to touch base with either your physician or a travel clinic.* (Peter Contini, M.D., 8 years experience)

Chapter 10

The Flight Process: Planning Ahead for a Smooth Flight

1. Type up your itinerary, including confirmation numbers and important phone numbers for airlines, rental cars, and hotels (include the local numbers at your destination if in a foreign country). Leave a copy with a trusted friend or family member at home and put another copy in your luggage. Keep in mind that any information that is in your luggage will be seen by any number of people who are doing a security search of your luggage. Protect confidential information (credit card numbers, social security numbers, etc.)

> *One of the things I always say, no matter how short the trip, type up an itinerary. Even if it's just a long weekend...it doesn't have to be minute by minute, but in the itinerary you can have suggested things that you're going to do, what you're actually going to do. You can put onto the itinerary the confirmations, the rates, the telephone number you called to get the hotel, to get the car reservation. It's all in one place.* (Brenda Elwell, Single Parent Travel Expert, 40 years experience)

2. Make copies of your passport, leaving one copy with a trusted relative or friend at home, and carrying a copy with you as you travel. I also like to make a photocopy of the front and back of my credit cards and any other important information. (I also do this in everyday life in case my purse/wallet is lost or stolen, all the information is right there so I would know who to call and what my card numbers are – no matter where I am geographically.)

Just make sure not to carry this information in your purse or wallet!

3. Talk to your children about the game plan. Even 2-year-olds like to know what is going on. Make this age appropriate and involve their input.

> *Most successful trips are when kids are invested in the trip in terms of helping to pre-plan, looking up online to see the destination they're going, each of the children picking one fun thing that they really want to do, and mom and dad buying into it.* (Kathryn Sudeikis, CTC- Travel Agent, 35 years experience)

> *As soon as we discuss it and say we're going to do it, I have them go online with me. I show them pictures and tell them where we're going to go and . . . I keep on telling them. We . . . mention something about it every day until the event, and that's part of the excitement and preparation.* (Gilly, Traveling Mom, 6 years experience)

Another mom I interviewed stated she prefers to wait until the day before to tell her daughter of their travel plans.

All children are different as are parenting styles and family life. Please take into consideration how your child will react.
Some children do much better being prepared and involved, while for others this may increase anxiety because they do not understand time and why they are not leaving now instead of next month!
You know your children best.

---

4.   Research local customs and food, history of the area, and proper attire, and respect foreign cultures.

5. Pack appropriate clothing and dress your children well, as they will be treated with more respect than if they were in shorts and T-shirts.

I always had them dress nice . . . a nice collared shirt, nice pair of pants. . . a blouse and a skirt, or a blouse and slacks . . . particularly if we traveled to a foreign country . Maybe not so much in this country, but definitely overseas, and particularly in third-world countries like Central and South America . . . people judge you by what you wear; they make an assumption about you. (Brenda Elwell, Single Parent Travel Expert, 40 years experience)

6. Airplanes tend to be cool; layer your clothing *and* your child's for comfort. However, keep in mind that installing the car seat, hauling luggage, and keeping two steps ahead of your child may make you uncomfortably warm! Layer, layer, layer!

7. Familiarize children with airplane travel. If a child is younger and this is his first plane trip, it can be a scary thing. Read them books about flying and airports so they can be familiar with the environment and process.

One book that I have found that is great for small children is Busy at the Airport:

Rebecca Finn's Busy at the Airport Book:

http://www.JetWithKidsClub.com/toys

I bought this book for my son at a bookstore in Rome. Even though the text is in Italian (the one above is in English), he LOVES to read through the book and turn the wheels making the luggage go round and the planes fly. This has been his favorite book and has been used many times in church to keep him entertained and quiet! (Anya's review)

Familiarize your children with airplane travel. If your child is young, under 10 and it's his or her first plane trip, it can be a scary thing . . . buy a book about an airplane trip, talk about check-in procedures. Explain how you fly above the clouds.

Jet With Kids:
Taking the Fear Out of Flying
WITH YOUR KIDS!

90

Yes, there's bathrooms onboard or little things that they don't think of. If you live near an airport, I suggested taking a child there for a reconnaissance visit, and to be prepared that if you frequently fly and become very blasé that that will not be the case with your child and you need to revel and enjoy in their enthusiasm and their million-and-one questions. Conversely, if you're a nervous flier then that's likely to rub off too, as well. (Brenda Elwell, Single Parent Travel Expert, 40 years experience)

a. "Shae By Air" DVD Toolkit

This great DVD toolkit is perfect for preparing young children for the flight process. The DVD was made specifically for toddlers, designed with their development in mind, walking them through the process of packing, airport security, the boarding process, sitting in their seat, what to expect during flight, popping ears, landing, etc. It is a toolkit as it also contains a simple packing list for toddlers so they can pack their own carry-on bag.

I love to meet other parents who see a need for something and instead of complaining about it, they create a product or solution.

As a traveling mother, Scotty Kober was frustrated by the lack of age appropriate tools available to prepare her toddler, Shae, for an upcoming international flight to Paris. She identified this need and created a professional, entertaining, and educational video that holds a toddlers' attention, but is informative for really- any age traveler!

I recently contacted Scotty and asked her about her motivation for creating this wonderful tool. She states, *"My whole point is how can we as parents expect children to be well behaved if they don't know what to expect and what is expected of them??*

That was the question I was trying to answer with the product. What was I hoping to find and buy for Shae before our international trip that would prepare her for such a long flight?

I knew I wanted it to be something visual, so she could recognize and emulate - to SEE a good example set, to HEAR the process explained in words that encouraged, not scared her, and to DO something - to be a part of the trip. Helping pack makes it her trip too, not just something she is dragged along on. "

Scotty explains these points about the DVD toolkit:

It is NOT:
- just a movie
- for parents

It IS:
- a toolkit - for toddlers

It contains:

1) Audio/visual (movie, at a length that keeps toddlers' attention, which according to child development experts is under 20 minutes)

2) Tactile (packing list and luggage tags)

3) Role model behavior (children are able to mimic what they see on the screen), and it's shot at their height in live action (not a cartoon, which is more difficult for them to relate to)

4) A video message for parents
** While this product will ultimately help parents by virtue of what it shows their children, the product is actually FOR toddlers.

Jet With Kids:
Taking the Fear Out of Flying
WITH YOUR KIDS!

92

"Shae By Air" DVD Toolkit allows your child to see and hear ahead of time what they will experience before and during a flight. Parents reviewing this product often comment on how their children become attached to the video and refer to Shae as someone they relate to as they complete the flight process.

This is a fabulous tool for children –don't miss it!

You can find this DVD toolkit at:

www.JetWithKidsClub.com/tools

b. <u>Role-play the flight process -children tend to behave better when they know what to expect.</u> I loved the example that Renée, a retired flight attendant, gave when she helped her neighbor, commercial pilot and traveling mom Carole, prepare for flying with her triplets. Renée volunteered to role-play with the triplets so they would recognize the flight process once they arrived at the airport.

Renée started the role-play by arranging the family living room into a make-believe airport terminal and airplane:

For the plane, they set up chairs and had an aisle between the chairs. The triplets helped to pack their individual backpacks and then they got in the car and pretended to drive to the airport, park and walk into the terminal.

They then had to role-play the act of going through security, practicing taking their shoes off and putting their belongings on a "moving belt". They were told about how the machine would take a picture to see what's inside their bags. They then picked up their backpacks and pretended to walk to the gate. Renée, role playing as the gate agent, asked for their boarding passes as they walked onto the plane. They sat in the chairs and applied a belt (clothing belt) as a seat belt around the chair that they then buckled.

Looking the part of a flight attendant as she was wearing her uniform, she talked them through the safety procedures of buckling the seat belt. She made the announcement for take off and instructed them to keep their belts on. Once the plane was in the air, they were served beverages in small plastic cups from a cart that Renée walked down their little aisle, giving them choices of what they could drink.

She then made the announcement that they were about to land, and how they needed to make sure their seat belts were still fastened. Once they landed, they were instructed on how to put their backpacks on and get off of the plane. Carole, their mom, stated she left the "plane" set up until the day they actually flew and they played many hours in that living room, "practicing" for their adventure by playing airplane.

When they actually did take that flight, they were prepared and had fun, looking forward to things like security and buckling their seat belts – things that they had practiced.

Children do amazingly well when given a chance and some proper preparation. If the parent or guardian preps them on the procedure, it is somewhat familiar to them and they know how they are expected to act. As is true with every area of a child's life, they will always do better when they understand what their boundaries are as well as expected behavior.

c. <u>Teach your children how to make direct eye contact and have a firm handshake.</u> With practice, even a child as young as two can be taught how to properly greet an adult.
    When you meet people, giving them a direct gaze . .
    .   answering   them   politely,   with   a   firm

Jet With Kids:
Taking the Fear Out of Flying
WITH YOUR KIDS!

94

handshake...shows respect for other people, and they in turn, will respect you. (Brenda Elwell, Single Parent Travel Expert, 40 years experience)

8. <u>Keep your family healthy.</u> A sick child is no fun for anyone and can cause a trip to be canceled or ruined. There are a few good things that you can do in preparation for your flight:

a. <u>Boost the immune system</u>. Some travelers use products to help naturally boost their immune system.
- Airborne Effervescent Tablets. **(http://JetWithKidsClub.com/health)**

- My family has seen great benefits from drinking juices like Goji Juice and Ning Xia Red Juice. For more information on these juices, email me at info@JetWithKids.com.

b. <u>Minimize your child's playtime with other children the week before traveling.</u> Many times small children rapidly spread germs, and it may take a few days for an illness to appear.

c. <u>Keep your bodies healthy and strong with proper nutrition, good sleep, decreased stress, and exercise.</u>

d. <u>Wash hands with soap!</u>

e. <u>ALWAYS TRY OUT NEW MEDICATIONS AHEAD OF TIME</u>.
Some over-the-counter medications like Benadryl and cough syrups can have the opposite of their desired effect (paradoxical), and 37,000 feet in the air is not a good place to have a hyper child—or worse yet, an allergic reaction.

9. <u>Plan your airport transportation wisely and ahead of time.</u> As you arrange your ride to the airport, be sure to allow enough time. Keep in mind traffic patterns, possibilities of traffic delays, lines at

airport, and getting through security. If you are having someone drop you off, figure in extra time in case they are running late. As Gate Agent A points out, at certain airports, there can be more than one required security line for your bags—**always allow extra time!**

Consider a hotel stay-and-park. I like this option since it adds to the vacation by taking away some stress and giving us more time. Check out the hotels around the airport. Many of them will offer a park and stay option. This means if you stay one night either before you leave on your trip or when you return, you can park your car there while you are away.

Hotels we stay at allow us to park free for up to 10 days. When you add up the cost of parking at the airport or gas for someone to drop you off and pick you up, it can get close to the cost of a hotel. The nice thing about the hotel option is that you actually get something in addition to the parking. This is especially nice if you live far from the airport or if you have an early morning flight and don't want to deal with traffic. By staying at a hotel that is near the airport, you can take the hotel shuttle and arrive at the airport in a few short minutes and not worry about traffic. And the hotel stay can start your vacation a night early!

10. Prepare your luggage.
    a) Luggage tags/bag ID. Have you noticed how few people mark their bag so that they are easily identifiable? Many bags are black and look alike. It is a good idea to attach a unique luggage tag or something eye-catching so that your luggage is easy to spot. You do not want to have to wait at baggage claim any longer than necessary, especially when you are traveling with children.

    b) Name and address label. Gate Agent B, (28 years airline experience) who handles baggage for a major airline, states that it is more important to put your name and phone number on your luggage than an address. He states that especially with how busy everyone is at the airport, your phone number is really the information that

Jet With Kids:
Taking the Fear Out of Flying
WITH YOUR KIDS!

96

they need. And since most people have a cell phone in their traveling party, it is more likely that they will be able to contact you.

c) <u>Put contact information on the inside of your bag as well</u>. Tags can get ripped off in transport, leaving your bag unidentifiable.

d) <u>Pay attention to luggage weight restrictions!</u> We flew on a European carrier for an unbelievably low price within Europe. However, their luggage restrictions were *very* strict. I am told that is how they make their money—since they charge for weight overage on carry-ons as well as checked luggage. Overage charges can add up quickly and any "good deal" that you got on your ticket can disappear into luggage fees. Since I knew in advance their very limited options for carry-on, I was still able to fly for one very low fare!

e) <u>Also be prepared to have a small bag inside your carry-on</u> filled with absolute essentials such as medication, diapers, wipes, and food. This is in case the flight is full or, if for security purposes, your carry-on is not allowed on board. It does not pay to argue, since that will only increase the tension and stress. Just be prepared with alternative luggage solutions!

f) <u>Some major carriers have new weight restrictions,</u> allowing a maximum of 50 pounds per piece of checked luggage. Please check with your airline in advance.

g) <u>Have children help pack their own backpack,</u> as they tend to be more responsible for items and are able to help carry it. A roller bag is nice for them to pull, and a backpack is nice to wear. If you can find a combination roller/backpack, you have more options when they get tired.

Luggage for Kids:
http://www.JetWithKidsClub.com/luggage

Gate Agent Victoria says it is very important that families arrive at the airport prepared. *"They really need to plan ahead, reserve their seats, board early, have name tags on all their luggage before they get to the airport, have id's available."* (Gate Agent Victoria, 23 years airline experience)

 **Child Safety**

Here are some general safety tips:

1. <u>Talk to your children (age appropriately) about not talking to strangers</u> and what to do if you get separated at any point during your trip. Include a copy of your itinerary and contact information in your child's bag.

2. <u>Dress your child in a noticeable color</u>. If you have multiple children, Beth McGregor of Traveling With Kids advises that you dress them all in the same "team colors." For instance, they would all wear red shirts and jeans. This makes it easy to do a "nose count" and also helps to find a lost child.

3. <u>I like to bring along a current photo of my child</u> and have each adult in our traveling party carry one of him as well. It may be difficult to describe a lost child when you are panicking. Also make sure that it is easily accessible. A photo is a quick tool to help locate a missing child. Also make a mental note what color clothes your child is wearing on the day of travel.

4. <u>Explain to your child whom you feel it is okay for them to talk to</u> if they feel uncomfortable around a stranger or are lost (someone in uniform—airline employee, security, or police).

Jet With Kids:
Taking the Fear Out of Flying
WITH YOUR KIDS!

98

5. <u>Educate your children about not talking to strangers</u>, wandering off, or interfering with other passengers who desire to rest, read, or work during their flight.

6. <u>Teach your child to say your first and last name</u>, or the name of the adult with whom he's traveling. Even just the first name can be helpful.

7. <u>Traveling with a toddler is a lot more challenging when they like to wander off.</u> Airports are filled with people, and if you are preoccupied with getting through the process of security, checking in, buying snacks, it is easy to quickly lose track of that little wanderer.

Helpful Products For Use In The Airport

I loved the Baby Bjorn carrier to allow me hands-free transport through the airport. My son enjoyed the security and muffled noises as he was snuggled against my chest. Just keep in mind that you will need to remove your baby from the carrier when you're going through security in the airport. Refer to the links below to purchase the Baby Bjorn that best meets your needs:

Baby Bjorn Active Carrier with Lumbar Support
& Baby Bjorn City:

<u>http://www.JetWithKidsClub.com/transport</u>

> *I absolutely loved the Baby Bjorn that we had for my infant son. Hands free travel is great and having him snuggled in next to me gave us both a feeling of calm. Especially when he flew as a newborn, I found this to be a great way to protect him from all of the germs on hands of well meaning, but not always health conscious strangers that wanted to touch him. I did not have the Active Carrier, and I believe it offers more lumbar support – which would have been nice especially as my son got older and weighed more. (Anya's review)*

The baby sling wrap is a very popular way to keep your baby snuggly close, and does not take up much room in your carry-on. Even though the wrap is approved for newborns and children up to 45 lbs., most parents like to use it up to 35lbs.

Refer to the following link to purchase the *Moby Wrap* **(http://www.JetWithKidsClub.com/transport)**, a highly recommended sling for traveling with your baby:

> *I have talked to many, many mothers who looked so comfortable with their content baby inside a wrap. Recently in Hawaii, I spoke with a traveling grandma who said her daughter was asked about it ALL the time, so much that she was thinking of printing out some information about it to hand out! These look very versatile and babies always seem happy and many times are sleeping in them. This can be great for the breastfeeding mother, to offer privacy in public areas of the airport.*
> *(Anya's review)*

Most recently I have used the Ergo Baby Carrier for transporting my 30 pound toddler through London and Vienna.

Ergo Baby Carrier:

(http://www.JetWithKidsClub.com/transport)

> *I was skeptical that any carrier would support the weight of my 30 lb. toddler without some serious strain on my back. The Ergo Baby Carrier is amazing! It was designed by a mom unable to find a carrier that fit her needs. My son slept hours in the carrier as I walked through the city without pain or strain on my back and shoulders. I am excited to use this carrier for future trips.*
> *(Anya's review)*

I love to hear about people who see a need for something and then take the time and effort to create it.

Jet With Kids:
Taking the Fear Out of Flying
WITH YOUR KIDS!

100

That is exactly the story behind my very favorite children's travel products website. I instantly liked the layout and the colors and products of this website. When I called with a question, traveling mom Beth McGregor, answered the call herself after putting her son down for an afternoon nap.

We instantly connected, traveling moms with a love and passion for showing our children the world. She told me the story of how she and Lorna Evenden, also a traveling mom and her neighbor, saw a need for one complete website for children's travel products. As traveling moms, they knew that there were quality products out there dedicated to children's travel, but were frustrated that they had to search in different catalogs and on different websites to find them. This is what prompted them to start their own website. They welcome parent feedback and suggestions and have a wide variety of products for children, categorized by event and age.

Throughout this resource, I have listed many of their products, with web links to make it easier for busy parents who want to purchase them. I have also included my personal reviews for many of the products.

They offer gift certificates to their site:

(http://www.JetWithKidsClub.com/gifts)

This is a great gift for any traveling family!

They also have a gift finder that allows someone to enter the gender of the child as well as the age for appropriate gift ideas. Whether you are traveling around the world or around town, their site helps make traveling with kids fun and safe.

Here are some great products to keep children near, find them when they wander off, and help others return them to you:

- Two in One Harness Buddy
  (http://www.JetWithKidsClub.com/airport) Have you ever not wanted to use the harness option because you thought it cruel or worried about what others said?

This is a cute, fun alternative to the plain child harness, and gives parents comfort knowing that their child will not wander off in a crowded area. The harness is a stuffed animal backpack that attaches to your child, and the tail of the animal can be looped around your wrist.

My son has the puppy harness and loves to buckle it himself. I have found that it can be very helpful to alleviate fears about going through security. He tends to focus on being the caretaker of "Puppy" and tells his little puppy that he has to go for a ride on the belt if he wants to go on the airplane. My son is usually so focused on getting through the metal detector to see puppy come through the other side of the belt, that he is not intimidated by the metal detector itself.

The puppy harness is put away with his suitcase when we are not traveling, so he is happy to see it when we get it out. He also uses the puppy as something to hug on the airplane (and can double as a pillow) – it is really soft!

Many people comment on how cute it is – and it really does help when my hands are full to feel that "tail" around my wrist. When we walk through the airport, I hold my son's hand, even though the tail is around my wrist. I keep him close and he is used to that. That way when I have to let go of his hand, he tends to stay close from habit, but if he gets distracted, I still have the tail of the puppy around my wrist.

(Anya's review)

- Giggle Bug Toddler Tracker (http://www.JetWithKidsClub.com/airport) This product is a 2-part device. One part is a device similar to a key-less-entry car remote that is kept with you. The other part is the ladybug that attaches to your child's pants or back of his shirt. If your child is lost, you push the panic button on your device, and your child's ladybug unit starts beeping. It's a great way to ensure your child does not get too far away in a crowded place.

Jet With Kids:
Taking the Fear Out of Flying
WITH YOUR KIDS!

102

- <u>Whos Shoes Child ID</u> and <u>ID Contact Card</u> **(http://www.JetWithKidsClub.com/airport)** These products give you a place to attach your contact information to your child. This is a great way for authorities to know whom to contact in case of an emergency.

I use the Whos Shoes Child ID. I feel strongly that if I should get separated from my son, someone could immediately notify me when finding him. I write my name and my husband's name as well as our cell phone numbers as the contact information. While traveling, my toddler son is good about keeping them on his shoe (it Velcro's through the laces), but once we return home, he takes them off when he is bored in his car seat on the way home from the airport. He is usually too interested in his new surroundings to notice them while in the airport. The photo online shows a pink tag, but my son received a blue one when I ordered. I don't know if there is an option of color. (Anya's review)

Once again, being prepared many times means a better trip for all!

Chapter 11

The Flight Process: Packing

"My uncle told me this once . . . if you're going to plan a trip, pack everything you're going to bring. Walk around your block once and see how tired you are at the end . . . if you're not tired then bring it, if you are [tired, then repack!] . . . because when [you're traveling], you are carrying your suitcases around." (Reservations Agent, 7 years experience)

"You have to be able to walk 2 long blocks with all your luggage. You have to be self-sufficient. If you can't do that, then you have to leave some of it at home, because there will be a time when you have to walk 2 long blocks with all of your luggage!" (Brenda Elwell, Single Parent Travel Expert, 40 years experience)

 Carry-On

Here is what I have learned about the amount of carry on luggage:

> **LESS IS BEST!**
> Be prepared, pack light but smart, don't bring unnecessary items onboard! I cannot stress that enough!!! But at the same time,
> you do need to be prepared!

Put a checklist in your suitcase and leave it there for the next trip. Do not make this more work than it has to be. Update the list when you get home noting what you could have left out and what you needed. Keep in mind that with children, age and development change, and need to be taken into consideration each time you fly.

Jet With Kids:
Taking the Fear Out of Flying
WITH YOUR KIDS!

104

Please check the TSA prohibited items website for up-to-date regulations.

http://www.tsa.gov

With the recently heightened security, there are new things that are prohibited onboard. Realize that this is for your protection and not to make your life more difficult. It is your responsibility to check before the day of departure with TSA for up-to-date restrictions.

The items that I recommend should *not* be packed in a carry-on if they are prohibited by TSA. It is against the law to bring prohibited items even to the point of security!

If you notice that liquids are banned, and you want to bring something like Infants' Tylenol on board, bring a note from your physician that states it is necessary. However, the TSA supervisor *will* have the final say on whether or not it is allowed.

> **All prescription medications *must* be properly labeled and in the correct container (with prescription label attached).**

Following are items that I have found to be helpful to pack in your carry-on. However, safety and the rules of the TSA come first. Purchase liquids that your child will need onboard during take off, while you are in the boarding area. If you forget, ask a flight attendant for a beverage for your child once you get on board - do not wait until the plane is taking off.

Here is a list of items I like to include in my carry-on:

Happy Traveler Family Gear Bag:

http://www.JetWithKidsClub.com/carryon

> *I use the* <u>Happy Traveler Family Gear Bag</u>
> *as my carry-on and love the separate and spacious*
> *compartments. In fact, a TSA Agent once commented*
> *on it, saying he liked it and all the compartments*
> *made his job easier. He then finished by saying that a "mom must*
> *have designed it!" (Anya's review)*

1. Documentation:

a) <u>ID</u> (yours, and for your child – photocopy of birth certificate, school, or state ID)

b) <u>Passports</u> (yours and ALL children if flying internationally)

2. Small Wallet:

a) <u>Cash</u>: Bring small bills – at least $20 to cover small fees like:

i) <u>Curbside check in for your bags</u>. I have found that this is a wonderful alternative to the long lines at the ticket counter. Online check in 24 hours in advance and get your seat assignments, then check your bags at the curb. It is common for the fee to be around $2/checked bag. Plus figure a tip on top of that. It can add up quickly, but standing in line just to check a bag at the counter starts your trip off with unnecessary waiting.

ii) <u>Purchasing snacks or meals on the flight.</u> Most of them cost around $5, and flight attendants prefer correct change. Although I do recommend bringing your own snacks, there are some healthier meal choices now available for purchase in flight. On a recent flight, my son loved the grapes, crackers, raisins, and cantaloupe.

3. **Itinerary:**

a) <u>Flight Info, Tickets</u> (Flight #s, airline phone #, confirmation #)

b) <u>Rental car, hotel, vacation rental, phone numbers</u>

4. **Prescription drugs:** (You never know how long you may be delayed on the plane.)

a) <u>If children have prescription medication, pack it in the carry-on (asthma inhaler, EPI pen, insulin, etc.).</u> Always have it available—you never know if you will need it!

b) <u>Prescription Drugs *must* be labeled properly to go through security and customs.</u>

c) <u>If medication needs to be refrigerated, do not rely on airlines to take care of this for you.</u> There is a product that is a "cooler pack" that keeps medication cool during travel. Read the instructions for product before use.

Frio Cool Pouch:
http://www.JetWithKidsClub.com/health

Peter Contini, M.D. also recommends bringing along:

- <u>Snacks for diabetics and for children who have specific food allergies;</u>

- <u>Medical Records</u>—depending on where you are going, and depending on if there is a chronic problem. This can be very helpful to a treating physician—a brief listing of problems is fine.

As you would with any confidential information, protect this and be responsible for keeping it in your possession.

5. Over the Counter Medications
**Please check the TSA website (http://www.tsa.gov) the day of departure to verify what is allowed and what is prohibited.

> **Always consult with your physician**
> **before administering medication or supplements to your child.**

Some travelers give Children's Benadryl or children's cough syrup to help children sleep during the flight. There can be a paradoxical—opposite—effect of these medications (make child hyperactive). **Try this out ahead of time!**

   a) Children's/Infants' Tylenol

   b) Children's/Infants' Motrin

   c) Children's/Infants' Mylicon (different food, anxiety, combined with expansion of the abdominal air at 37,000 feet can cause uncomfortable tummies)

   d) Children's/Infants' Benadryl: Peter Contini, M.D. states that it may be important "especially if you have a younger child who hasn't been exposed to all foods in case they have an allergic reaction."

6. Camera and Photos:
   a) Camera: Great for trips and fun to have photos of your flight

   b) Current Photo of Child: I like to bring along a photo of my child and have each adult in our traveling party carry this. **It is difficult to describe a lost child when you are panicking.** A photo is a quick tool to help locate a missing child.

   c) Variety of Fun Photos: (double stick tape these photos on the back of the seat in font of you – helps with preventing kicked seats and also is great entertainment!)

Jet With Kids:
Taking the Fear Out of Flying
WITH YOUR KIDS!

108

7. **Diapers & Diaper Cream:** Bring more than you calculate you will need (delays, diarrhea, etc. can happen!).

    a) <u>Be prepared to change diapers in your lap or seat since not all airplane bathrooms have changing facilities.</u> (It's good to have a pad to lay your child on)

    b) <u>If your child is very young and potty training is in process or just completed, do not take the risk.</u> Go back to diapers for the flights, as it is better to be safe!

    c) <u>Pull-up diapers are a nice option for the older child, as these are easier to change while they are standing up.</u>

Pull-Up Diapers:

http://www.JetWithKidsClub.com/carryon

    d) <u>Bring a larger zip lock or a scented plastic bag to enclose the diaper.</u> Please do not ask the flight attendants to dispose of them unless they are well enclosed and you are unable to do so yourself.

Bag It Plastic Bags:

http://www.JetWithKidsClub.com/carryon

 These bags are great as they attach onto your luggage and are easy to access. They work well for disposing of diapers and trash while traveling. I use them while out and about in town as well as across the world.
(Anya's review)

8. **Change of clothes (or 2):** Bring them for your child *and* for yourself (spills and vomit do happen!). Bring comfortable clothing for the children: a thin pair of sweatpants will do the trick, and a light jacket is good in case there's a draft. Bring a

sweater along to layer clothes since planes can be cold even in summer.

9. **Variety of snacks:** Bring healthy snacks—granola bars, crackers, raisins, Cheerios. **Apply these tips according to what is age and developmentally appropriate for your child. Do not give your child foods that present a choking hazard.**

> a) Try to avoid sugar and junk foods.

> b) Do not *count* on the airlines to provide your food—you will be happier that you can eat *when* you want, *what* you want!

Bring alternative food since your toddler may refuse to eat what the airline has to offer. Beth, a traveling mom, makes things like bow tie pasta with Parmesan cheese ahead of time and puts it into a thermos.

10. **Sippy cup:** It's a good idea to bring this, even if you're not using it at home anymore. You'll have fewer spills. Keep in mind that it will need to be empty when you're boarding the plane, to comply with TSA rules.

Sigg Switzerland Bottle:

http://www.JetWithKidsClub.com/snacks

Sippy Cup:

http://www.JetWithKidsClub.com/snacks

11. **Extra pacifiers/bottles:** Extras are a good idea in case one drops on the floor or is lost.

Jet With Kids:
Taking the Fear Out of Flying
WITH YOUR KIDS!

110

12. **Quiet toys:** Avoid bringing toys that are loud, sharp, or have many parts.

a) Here are some ideas to consider:
(**http://www.JetWithKidsClub.com/toys**)
-Books (both new and favorites)
-The Activity Book
-Coloring/Activity Books
-The Sticker Book
-Finger Puppets
-A Doll or Bear
-CD Player with Headphones
-Comic Books
-Crossword Puzzles
-Small Cars/ Trucks
-Disposable Camera
-Crayons and Coloring Book
-Rescue Truck Book
-Suction Cup Critters

MAGNETIC TINS
(**http://www.JetWithKidsClub.com/toys**)
Magnetic Fun Tins - Disney
Magnetic Fun Tins - ABC & 123
Magnetic Fun Tins - Car, Planes & Trains
Disney Princess Travel Tins
Magnetic Fun Tins - House
Large Imaginetics USA Maps
Large Imaginetics Tonka
Large Imaginetics Doll House
Large Imaginetics Fire Station
Large Imaginetics Airport
Large Imaginetics Pet Vet
Large Imaginetics Bob The Builder

b) Some moms like to wrap the toys individually in wrapping paper or a brown bag to make it more fun to open. It helps to hide favorite toys for a couple weeks before you bring them along. The Treasure Bag (**http://www.JetWithKidsClub.com/toys**) is a small backpack that comes with gift-wrapped toys that you can give to your child throughout the trip. This can be a great way to keep them busy with new activities.

The treasure bag is recommended for children 3-8 years of age. My son (who is 2) played with many of the toys in it on our last flight. These small gift-wrapped toys were a perfect way to keep him entertained. Included with the small backpack was a card that listed the items that were in the bag. When ordering, specify the gender of the child. Some of the toys that he really liked were the mini chalkboard and eraser, the mini car, and the notebook and crayons. (Anya's review)

13. Portable DVD player/Gameboy (http://www.JetWithKidsClub.com/toys):

All electronic devices are to be used only during the cruise portion of the flight as they may interfere with the aircraft's navigational system during takeoff and landing.

a) Bring sufficient battery power.

b) When watching a DVD, be courteous to those around you and use headphones. If two children are watching it, use an adapter that allows two headsets to be plugged in. You may not think it is annoying to hear the buzz of Thomas the Train noises, but the person next to you may need to rest or work and that little bit of noise can interfere with concentration or relaxation.

Headphone Splitter:
http://www.JetWithKidsClub.com/toys

Okay, and then enter into the world of iPods! I am not there yet, but the video iPods look to be an incredible way to entertain the whole family! Download favorite TV shows, music, photo albums, etc. If you are not familiar

Jet With Kids:
Taking the Fear Out of Flying
WITH YOUR KIDS!

112

with them, ask a teenager, I am sure they know more about this than I (my son is only a toddler!) do. I am including links to both the iPod and the video iPod.

Video iPod:
http://www.JetWithKidsClub.com/toys

iPod:
http://www.JetWithKidsClub.com/toys

c) Save the DVD player/Gameboy/iPod for when you really need it. View it like a treat and instead interact with your children while in flight. According to Brenda Elwell, single-parent travel expert, the parents who have the most trouble are those who pull out their book as soon as they get on the flight and ignore their kids.

14. **Hand Sanitizer Wipes:** These are handy even for the older child. Things tend to get sticky or spilled! Plus it is nice to wipe down the tray table and your seat environment. And of course, you need wipes for the diaper change. (I put the wipes in the seat pocket when I sit down so I don't have to search for them when I need them.)
Hand & Face Wipes:
http://www.JetWithKidsClub.com/health

15. **Ziploc storage bags:** These are invaluable on a trip of any kind with a child!
Ziploc Bags:
http://www.JetWithKidsClub.com/snacks

16. **Tissues:** It's horrible to need a tissue and not have one, or need to wait until the seat belt sign is turned off before you can go get one!

Pocket Tissues Perfect for Traveling:
http://www.JetWithKidsClub.com/health

I put tissues in several places since you never know when you might need them. I even include them in my son's little roller bag or backpack in an easily accessible area. (Anya's review)

17. **Small light blanket/small pillow:** Sometimes these aren't offered by the airline, and even if they are, they're not very sanitary.

Travel Pillow:
http://www.JetWithKidsClub.com/carryon

Cradler Head Support Travel Pillow:
http://www.JetWithKidsClub.com/carryon

Travel Blanket/Pillow:
http://www.JetWithKidsClub.com/carryon

18. **Chewing gum:** Gum is great for older children (age appropriate) and adults to chew during ascent and descent.

19. **Glasses/Sunglasses**

20. **Chapstick/Sample Size Hand Lotion:** Remember to put bottle of lotion in quart size bag to declare at TSA.

Unequivocally you need to be sure to pack patience and be prepared. And be prepared means making sure that you have something to keep every child with you busy on their own steam and with age-appropriate activities. (Kathryn Sudeikis, CTC-Travel Agent, 35 years experience)

21. **Any additional carry on items specific to your family's needs.**

Jet With Kids:
Taking the Fear Out of Flying
WITH YOUR KIDS!

114

For international travel, Gate Agent Victoria recommends the following,

> *I would definitely bring your own blankets because aircrafts are often cold. Bring sweaters or sweatshirts for your children, comfortable shoes, shoes that they can slip on and off. And I would make certain that their immunizations are all up-to-date and that you check out the health advisory for the country that you're visiting prior to going there.* (Gate Agent Victoria, 23 years experience)

 **Checked Baggage**

Since the new TSA rules prohibit liquids in your carry-on, prepare to buy some extra zip lock bags! Use them also to pack perfume and any other liquids that have to go in your checked luggage.

Also, check the **weight restrictions** ahead of time as they are always changing.

> **Some airlines have now lowered the restriction to a maximum of 50 pounds per checked bag. Check with your airline, as they *will* enforce these weight limits and can charge hefty fines!**

Luggage can get heavy fast, and you don't want to face more fees just because you packed one bag heavier than the others. It is easy to get an idea of what your bag weighs by standing on a scale without it and then with it and subtracting the difference for an estimate, or you can purchase a luggage scale.

****Realize that with the increased security measures,
there has been an increase in the amount of checked luggage.**

**With this increase, there is a greater chance of lost luggage. Carry any
essential items with you and protect yourself with travel insurance in case
your luggage doesn't arrive with you!**

<u>For a FREE Quote, Click on the Insure My Trip image at</u>

<u>http://www.JetWithKidsClub.com/links</u>

Chapter 12

The Flight Process: Check-In

Always take responsibility for your flight process. Verify all of your documentation—correct name, destination, and frequent flier number ahead of time.

 Online Check-In

> **Starting at twenty-four hours before your flight, you are allowed to check in online and obtain your boarding passes from the comfort of your home (while your children are sleeping or playing), avoiding the long lines at the airport.**

This option is fabulous when you have children, especially since it many times eliminates one of the long lines you would have had to stand in at the airport.

To check in online, go to your airline's website home page and follow the easy instructions to print your boarding pass. Make sure that your printer is working, since you will need to print your boarding pass.

Some of the other things you can do while checking in online:
- Change or obtain a seat assignment
- Enter your frequent flier number (this must be entered into your reservation before you fly to get credit for that flight)

- Obtain upgrades, if available, for certain frequent flier levels, or sometimes purchase the upgrade to first or business class
- Make changes to your flight
- Select how many pieces of checked luggage you will bring

One time my printer wasn't working, and I discovered that I was able to check in online, make any needed changes (seat assignments, upgrades, etc.) and then print my boarding pass at the kiosk when I arrived at the airport.

Airport Check-In

If you checked in online, you will need to check your luggage either at the curb or inside at the ticket counter.

* Keep your checked baggage stub in a safe place, as you may need it to claim your luggage or to report delayed/misplaced luggage.

Expect to pay a fee in order to check bags curbside. The tip is now in addition to the actual fee that goes to the airline. Some low-cost airlines are not charging at this time, and the tip is still expected and worth it. Be prepared with small bills for unexpected expenses such as this.

> **If you need to make changes that aren't allowed online, or if you are checking in an unaccompanied minor, you will need to check-in at the airport ticket counter due to documentation requirements. If you are flying internationally, you may check-in online, but you will also need to check-in at the airport because of these documentation requirements.**

Have your documentation (tickets, IDs—passports, if international) out and ready for the ticket agent. If possible, I like to stand in line while my husband walks with my son nearby. They then join me when I get toward the front of the line. It can be too difficult

Jet With Kids:
Taking the Fear Out of Flying
WITH YOUR KIDS!

118

for small children to stand in line not moving and not understanding what is going on.

 **Kiosks**

Many of the airlines are also encouraging the use of the self-check-in monitors. They are simple and self-explanatory and can save you time. Most of the time you will be asked to insert a credit card or frequent flier card for identification. The computer will walk you through the check-in process.

> **If you are checking luggage, the kiosk or online check-in will ask you how many bags you are checking.**
> **If you select a number higher than what is allowed (most airlines allow two per ticketed passenger), you will be charged a fee.**

 **Gate Check**

As a parent traveling with small children, you will learn quickly the wonderful convenience of gate checking. This is when you can push your stroller to the door of the plane and they will check it and store it in the belly of the plane. They will then bring it back up on the jet way at your destination, and it will be available right outside of the door of the plane when you deplane.

A few things to note:

1. <u>Make sure to get a **gate-check tag** when you arrive at the gate</u>. Do not wait until you are boarding to ask for this (you will hold up the line and frustrate the gate agents).

2. <u>Always ask where you can pick up the stroller</u>—will it be brought to the jet way? I say this because in foreign countries they may have different locations.

3. That wonderful larger-than-life stroller that carries the infant car seat is great at home, but it is a nightmare in the airport and when traveling. It is too large and heavy for convenience. I say this because I was tempted to bring ours on a trip since I really loved it. Gate Agent Victoria told me how cumbersome it can be and instead how great the umbrella stroller was for flying. She also told me that the big, heavy strollers tend to get damaged more since the ramp agents have a difficult time lugging them up and down the stairs.

A **lightweight umbrella type stroller** that easily folds is a lifesaver when transporting your child, luggage, and carry-ons. Prior to our trip to Europe, I did a lot of research since I wanted a stroller that would be durable for the cobblestone streets.

I really like the **Maclaren Stroller (http://www.JetWithKidsClub.com/transport)**.

Beth McGregor of Traveling With Kids recommends the **Easy Walker Stroller (http://www.JetWithKidsClub.com/transport)**.

I really like the Maclaren Stroller. Many of my friends have different versions of it for traveling. I debated between the Triumph and the Quest. I am really glad that we chose the Quest since it reclines all the way, and the length of the seat extends so my son's legs are not dangling while sleeping. It is very lightweight and worked great over those cobblestone streets of Austria and Italy. It comes with a hood and rain cover. This rain cover worked great when it poured during our tour of the Colosseum in Rome, and my son was kept dry as he slept in the stroller under the rain cover. I also purchased the Maclaren stroller organizer bag that attaches to the back of the stroller. It holds water bottles and your belongings and has quite a large pocket that I used for our day trip stuff. The only things that I read that people didn't like about the Maclaren Quest stroller was that when you recline the seat you are unable to access the basket underneath to store things. I was fine with that since I had the bag on the back and I knew ahead of time what to expect. It is also rated for babies from age 3 months up to 55lbs., so it will last a while! (Anya's Review)

Jet With Kids:
Taking the Fear Out of Flying
WITH YOUR KIDS!

120

4. <u>Protect the stroller, its wheels, and other small parts that can</u> <u>break off</u>, by investing in **a sturdy bag to cover your stroller**. Put the **Padded Umbrella Stroller Bag (http://www.JetWithKidsClub.com/transport)** in the basket underneath the stroller when using the stroller. How awful would it be if you arrived at your destination and your stroller wheels were broken? You would have a broken stroller to CARRY and nowhere to put your child and certainly would not be equipped to get the stroller fixed in an unfamiliar area.

5. <u>Verify all of the info on all of your tags for gate check and</u> <u>checked luggage</u>. Employees are busy, and you need to take responsibility to confirm the destination. When gate-checking a stroller, make sure the connecting city is marked, as you will want to use the stroller during your connection.

Chapter 13

The Flight Process: Airport Security

> **With the recent heightened security, please check the TSA website (http://www.tsa.gov) before you travel for the most up-to-date list of prohibited items and for tips.**

For TSA guidelines on traveling with children and going through security: http://www.tsa.gov.

Probably a parent's number one question about security is how to best get through security with all of the "stuff" we bring along! Here are some great general tips for families going through security:

1. Explain the procedure to your children before you go—role-play at an age appropriate level. Tell your child about his belongings going through x-ray and how they will come out on the other side. Talk to him about taking his shoes off and putting them in the tray so the shoes can go through x-ray. (Some children may not realize what we take for granted, and they may think that they won't get their shoes back.) Explain to your child that they will need to walk through the "doorway that beeps".

As soon as children are old enough to walk, it is preferred that they walk alone through the metal detector. Explain ahead of time that you will not be able to walk through with them, but will be close behind or in front of them. If they are too frightened with the process, a parent or guardian can carry them through. This will vary as to the size of the child.

Jet With Kids:
Taking the Fear Out of Flying
WITH YOUR KIDS!

122

Example: A three-year-old girl can walk through by herself, but, if she is too frightened to do so, she may be carried through. If the metal detector goes off, they will be given an opportunity to go back and remove anything else they have on them, and then try again. If it still goes off, both individuals will be sent for extra screening.

2. <u>Look through your child's bag before you leave home</u>. In front of a waiting line and TSA personnel is not the place to find out that little Johnny brought along his jackknife. It will be confiscated, and a longer search will ensue—which guarantees more anxiety for all involved.

3. <u>At this point in time, you are allowed to bring breast milk, and formula if you are traveling with a baby or toddler.</u> If your child requires milk, you must provide it. Multiple times I have flown and not been able to purchase milk in the boarding area. The airplane itself does not have more than a few cartons of milk for passengers' coffee and you should not expect them to provide this for your child. Update: Liquids or gels, and pastes may now be carried on board an aircraft as follows: All containers must be under 3 oz. They must be placed in a 1-quart plastic, sealable, clear bag, and placed by itself in an x-ray bin. You may now purchase liquids, or gels in the waiting areas, and take them on board an airplane.

4. <u>Since the rules of security change frequently, check the TSA website, www.tsa.gov, for up-to-date regulations.</u> You can also check *average* wait times for that specific airport security on the following website:
  http://waittime.tsa.dhs.gov/index.html. Keep in mind that this does change and is usually just an average of historical wait times for that location.

5. <u>Explain the importance of following directions in the security line.</u> Tell your child not to even make jokes about bombs or weapons, since all comments are taken very seriously and will definitely lead to a longer search and questioning.

6. <u>If you have prescription medication along, be sure that it is properly labeled.</u> If you have any notes from a physician, have it easily accessible.

7. <u>It pays to think ahead...</u>If there is something that you absolutely need to take along, have documentation to support that in case you are questioned.

8. <u>Print out the section of the TSA website that pertains to something that you must carry onboard.</u> Do not assume that it will be okay. Also, ask to speak with a supervisor if you feel that you are being treated unfairly. And remain calm. In the case of security, do not assume anything.

*Remember that you are your child's advocate. As an RN who has taken care of sick passengers in medical emergencies onboard two different flights, I can tell you that things do happen, and you should never assume that the airline would have available what you need. Bring medications that your child may need if he gets sick.

9. <u>Have everyone wear shoes that are easy to slip off and on.</u> When your hands are full and time is short, you don't want to mess with difficult shoes.

10. <u>Take your child's and your shoes off before you reach the front of the security line</u>. Quite often, I hear people in line ask if they really need to take their shoes off. I have found that with heightened security, they do require all passengers, even babies, to have their shoes removed.

11. <u>Empty out all pockets of the stroller and your clothing and put contents into your bags *before* you get to the front of the security line.</u> Have your ID and boarding pass ready to show security. A great way to prevent losing your boarding pass and ID is to keep them in an <u>EZ Show Retractable ID Holder.</u> **(http://www.JetWithKidsClub.com/airport)**

Jet With Kids:
Taking the Fear Out of Flying
WITH YOUR KIDS!

124

 I used the EZ Show Retractable ID Holder to hold my boarding pass and ID on my last flight. It really did help since we had to show our boarding passes multiple times going through security and my hands were full holding my toddler and getting my laptop out of the bag. The ID holder clips right onto your belt loops or can be worn around your neck. (Anya's review)

12. <u>Take your child out of the stroller and collapse it down to its folded position so that it can go through the x-ray.</u>

13. <u>Some airports (mostly foreign) have separate lines for strollers; pay attention and follow directions.</u> I was told by an agent that if you are traveling as a solo parent with children or need assistance, you simply need to request it and someone will help you lift your bags onto the belt. I have not tried this yet, but it never hurts to ask if you need assistance with your bags.

14. <u>Everyone—including tiny babies—must go through security.</u> It is not allowed to hand your baby over to someone through the x-ray.

15. <u>TSA Personnel are *not* allowed to hold your child.</u> This is policy and should be respected.

 ## Questions Regarding Security Procedures

An anonymous Aviation Agent provided answers to these questions:

Are there any special considerations for TSA working with children? *There are no special considerations per se, however, we have to take each instance and see what is going to work best for both the adult and the children. We are expressly forbidden to hold, handle, or otherwise touch a baby or child in an assistive manner. Only if it is part of the screening process.*

Do all strollers and car seats need to go through the x-ray scanner? *This is not a requirement. Strollers and car seats, if able, should be sent through the x-ray when size is not a consideration. If a stroller, or car seat is too big, or is too difficult to be broken down to fit through the x-ray, it will be physically inspected. Key point:* **Not all airports use the same x-ray systems. These can vary in size, and what may fit in the x-ray at one airport, may not be able to fit at another.**

Do babies in carriers need to be taken out of the carriers? *As of today's date,* **all babies MUST be removed from carriers.** *The screening process for a baby is the same as it is for an adult, and they must be carried through the walk through metal detector by a parent, or traveling guardian. As with adults who may have medical conditions that do not allow them to walk through the metal detector, babies may have this same option. A full body pat down, or a hand held metal detector may be used to clear a passenger, regardless of age, or if they, or the parent or guardian request it. TSA is obligated under the law to grant the screening preferences of anyone. This process may change in the near future, as there will be a new operations guide out the first part of August [2006].*

Is there any assistance offered for the single parent? *Unfortunately, the TSA does not have a program, or anyone designated, to assist single parents. There are legal complications with this that could lead to a lawsuit, and the TSA does not allow the officers to handle babies in any way.*

What is the biggest issue that TSA has when dealing with families? *A lot of people have not done much homework before traveling. Especially families that rarely travel by air. Some get flustered at the screening process, and this can result in short tempers. We do our best to try and work with families who are traveling, but, once in a while, they may not understand what we are asking, or they misunderstand an instruction. Families who don't travel often should take the time to listen to what the screening officers are trying to explain to them so as to minimize delays and any hassles that may come about.*

Jet With Kids:
Taking the Fear Out of Flying
WITH YOUR KIDS!

126

What are your best tips for those families traveling with children? *The best tip I can offer is if you have Internet access, please visit http://www.tsa.gov and look over the section on travel tips. This will help not only parents, but also anyone who is traveling. Things like shoes are mentioned, along with a basic list of what cannot be allowed through a checkpoint.*

Are there places that you know of that have special lines designated for families? *As of today, I know of no airport that has a special line for families. I believe that this would be fairly cost prohibitive.*

Are there any special things for pregnant women to know about safety or tips? *Some women feel that they should not go through the walk-through metal detector while they are pregnant. This is entirely up to the individual, and the TSA will honor any such request. They would be submitted to a full-body pat down at this point. Ladies, wear comfortable, flat-soled shoes. This is the best advice I can give.*

Anything else? *I will add these couple of things: The x-ray machine will not harm medical x-rays once they are developed. Undeveloped x-rays must not be sent through the machine. Our x-ray systems are harmless to camera film up to 800 ISO. Any film that is 800 ISO or higher should not be sent through. Please ask for a hand inspection. A hand inspection must be granted if asked for. If anyone refuses to hand search film, or a camera containing film, please ask to speak to a supervisor. Digital cameras must be sent through the x-ray. There is no option to have these hand inspected. Jump drives: Please place these in your carry-on, or in a bin or bowl to be sent through the x-ray. The x-ray will not harm them. DO NOT keep them around your neck, or in your pocket and walk through the metal detector. This will erase, or at a minimum, over time, corrupt the files. The metal detector is an electromagnet field, and it's just the same as if you took a giant electric magnet and ran it over your video cassettes.*

"Kids like to watch what is on the x-ray screen when their bags go through. Although you can't get close to the monitor, you can point it out to kids." (Gilly, *Traveling Mom, 6 years experience*)

While writing this, I heard of a young woman who was forced to dump her baby's formula while going through security. I am sure that since TSA screeners are also human, there will be things like this that happen. I asked my anonymous source within TSA about a situation such as this and he responded with this:

Demand to speak to a supervisor . . . don't budge on this. A supervisor is the only one who can handle this type of behavior. If a passenger asks to speak to a supervisor, they have to get one for you. If the supervisor is busy, they still have to get them for you. If a supervisor doesn't help you, ask to speak to a screening manager. There is no excuse for someone dumping formula. That's a violation, and whoever did it should be reprimanded.

**Quick clarification: The statement above only applies if she had the child with her. If the child is not with her, and she is traveling alone, or with another adult, this would not be allowed.

I think the most important thing to remember about all of this is that it is for your safety. However, I do think that feedback is important, and if you feel you were treated unfairly or you want to compliment someone for a job well done, you may contact TSA at **TSA Contact Center toll-free at 1-866-289-9673** or you may e-mail TSA-ContactCenter@dhs.gov.

Remember, you are an example for your child. It never pays to get angry, violent, or be non compliant. Remain calm and if treated unfairly, speak with a supervisor. Keep in mind that a refusal to be screened will only result in more screening, more time, and more stress.

Jet With Kids:
Taking the Fear Out of Flying
WITH YOUR KIDS!

128

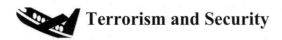 **Terrorism and Security**

It is sad that there even has to be a section on this, but many people have asked me about my thoughts. I flew cross-country the evening of September 10, 2001, and woke up in the morning to hear of the awful, horrifying events that took place September 11.

My thoughts and prayers go out to those families and friends and anyone that was harmed by the cruel actions of others. The travel industry was hit hard, and many times in my interviews people mentioned this. While I was writing this, more events have occurred in England, and terrorism is brought back to the front of the media reports.

My husband and I had a trip to Asia planned the month after the tragic act of terrorism of 9/11/2001. We chose to continue with our travel plans.

On that trip we met a couple in Thailand who changed forever what I thought about having children by their example and encouragement. We also met two couples from Canada, who became our wonderful lifelong friends. That trip changed my life.

My point in this is what I used to tell my patients in the hospital; you can't stop living or live in fear. Fear is a powerful thing and worse than any disease out there. It can paralyze the mind and body and rule more powerfully than the strongest leader.

I have a strong faith in my Lord and Savior, Jesus Christ, and death does not scare me. I know that life on earth is temporary and no amount of money, armor, or skill will prolong it if I am being called home. So I have chosen to make the decision to continue to travel, as well as to use caution when doing so. It is up to each and every person to have peace about his or her decisions, and that is something I respect. However, I think that we should recognize that there are many dangers in this life and to live in fear of them takes away from our quality of life.

"Do not be anxious about anything, but in everything, by prayer and petition, with thanksgiving, present your request to God. And the peace of God, which transcends all understanding, will guard your hearts and your minds in Christ Jesus." Philippians 4:6-7

**Travel with alertness, always keep safety in mind,
and be patient with those long lines at security;
they are in place to protect you.**

Chapter 14

The Flight Process: Your Departure Gate

 ## Finding Your Gate

Some people make the mistake of thinking that just because they made it through security with time left over, they have time to wander and shop. I recommend finding your gate first, leaving one person with the luggage in the gate waiting area and taking turns shopping, using the restroom, and walking up and down the terminal with your child.

Also, even as you are walking through the airport, your gate may change.

> **Always check the computer screens as you walk toward your gate to confirm your gate location.**

It is a stressful situation when you arrive at a gate only to find that it has been changed to one across the airport. (This happened to me!)

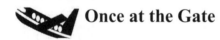 ## Once at the Gate

Boarding usually begins 45 minutes before international flights and 30 minutes before domestic flights. The gate agents will usually be working at the gate 45-60 minutes before departure to prepare for the flight. Do not interrupt them when they are working on something. Instead, wait until they make eye contact with you and are ready to assist you.

Please respect that they are trying to get the flight off on time and usually have many things to address.

> **It is a good idea to have someone in your party stay close to the gate until departure in case the airline makes a change: gate change, flight delay, flight cancellation, or calls your party to the counter for a message or seat change.**

As a parent who has a stroller, you will need to speak with the agent at the gate to obtain a gate-check tag. *Do not wait until you are boarding to do this, as you will hold up the line and the departure time.* The gate agents do *not* appreciate this delay, so plan ahead and immediately upon arriving at the gate, ask for a tag.

Now that I have said that, I must warn you that every agent works the flight a bit differently depending on their experience and what needs to be done to get the next flight out.

In the Rome airport, I asked for the gate tag and was told to wait. They then called out about 30 minutes later for all of the strollers and they tagged them all at once. So, as with every aspect of travel, be flexible and realize that your experience will be different every time.

> **Go with the flow, smile, smile, smile, breathe, breathe, breathe...**

Jet With Kids:
Taking the Fear Out of Flying
WITH YOUR KIDS!

132

Chapter 15

The Flight Process: Boarding

 **Pre-boarding**

It is interesting to hear who will advise you to pre-board and who says not to. Many flight attendants like to see that you are able to get the car seat secured and your belongings overhead before the rest of the passengers board.

Some reservations agents will tell you that you are not allowed to pre-board, and others say that you can. Some airlines are eliminating this practice. There are legitimate pros and cons to pre-boarding.

Pros:
It is nice to see an empty plane ahead of you and have a bit of time to get settled before the rush. You can take advantage of the whole row of seats being empty to secure the car seat next to the window, make sure that your carry-on items are easily accessible either under the seat or above you, and catch your breath before the other passengers board. Then you have time to get your child in the seat and settled with something to keep him occupied and look like a relaxed traveling pro as you watch the others struggle with their luggage and look for their seats.

Cons:
Twenty minutes of sitting still is hard for a young child, and that is before the plane has even moved. Twenty

minutes of time to walk around, up and down the airport hallways to let that last-minute energy out is worth a lot.

My two-year-old son usually is quiet the first 20 minutes we go someplace new. He looks around at everything new and is a bit shy as he surveys the situation and those around him. I like to have those 20 minutes be included in actual flight time or at least while we taxi out to the runway. The last thing I want is for him to be trying to get out of his seat due to boredom before we even leave the gate. I would also rather take him to the bathroom and change diapers or clothes in the airport bathroom, where I have more room to maneuver.

Many parents told me that they use this time in the airport to tire their children out. Brenda Elwell, traveling mom and single parent travel expert, liked to tell her children things they *could* do instead of always finding herself saying "no." She set boundaries and let them play until the seats in the gate area filled half full with people, and then they would come to her and read quietly until boarding.

This play in the airport can be very important to "let the steam out" and physically wear them down. Getting checked in and navigating the airport can build up stress internally as there is usually an underlying tension in a new, crowded situation.

> **It is also just as important to give them time to settle down before boarding the plane. Children (and adults!) do best when they have a "plan" and know what to expect.**

I have found that it works well when there are two adults traveling together and one boards first with all of the stuff, getting the car seat installed and the other keeps the child off the plane until near the end of boarding. Remember to each carry your own boarding pass to get on the plane!

Jet With Kids:
Taking the Fear Out of Flying
WITH YOUR KIDS!

134

(You can always nicely ask the gate agent if it is possible for one adult to pre-board and get the car seat installed to save time.)

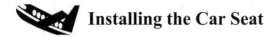 ## Installing the Car Seat

I write here from personal experience. Be careful not to get your hand caught in the back of the seat while trying to undo the seat belt! I have asked for a seat belt extender to help install the seat belt through the back of the car seat, making it easier to install and uninstall. However, I never count on the extender to be available.

Whether or not you use the seatbelt extender, make sure that the car seat is tightly secured!

Chapter 16

The Flight Process: Life on the Plane

 Emergency Preparedness

This is stuff nobody likes to think about, but it's necessary to review.

1. **Count the number of rows to the exit so you know where it is in case of an emergency—you may not have exit lighting!!**

> *Everyone should read the safety card, and...the parents should tell the children to read the safety card. Read it to your kids ... Also when you get on the plane, you need to know how many rows up is your emergency exit, forward and back, and you tell your children too . . . you don't want to scare them . . . but you keep in mind that in four rows above you and eight rows behind you is where the exit is.* (Renée, Retired Flight Attendant, 36 years experience)

I have actually found the safety card to be interesting entertainment for my son. He likes to point to things on it and we talk about what the people are doing.

I can tell you from my experience in emergency situations, whether in Code Blue hospital situations or the two in-flight medical emergencies (in which I was the only medical personnel onboard), people respond best to simple instructions.

Jet With Kids:
Taking the Fear Out of Flying
WITH YOUR KIDS!

136

Educating a child about what to do in an emergency could prove to be valuable as some adults may panic and not think clearly. A simple instruction from a child who reviewed the card might make the difference in the results of an emergency!

2. Pay attention to the safety video and what the flight attendants tell you.

> *Always pay attention to the safety video, and I would definitely say in an emergency . . . you need to count on yourself. Know where your exit is and take your child and go. You're in charge of your own safety. We're there to show you how to get off, but if something happens you and your child need to get off. Don't wait for somebody to carry you off; you need to be responsible.* (Flight Attendant A, 28 years airline experience)

3. If you are flying overseas, ask where the infant life vests are located. On one flight I was given one without asking, but on another flight I was told that it was in the closet. I do not want to wait for someone to help me find an infant vest in the case of an emergency.

4. Anyone that has flown has heard the explanation about applying your own oxygen mask before you assist others with applying theirs. This goes against our basic instinct as parents, until you understand the reasoning behind it. If the brain is not getting enough oxygen (hypoxia), the adult will get confused or may even pass out. If the adult has passed out, he is unable to help himself *or* the child.

Put your oxygen mask on first and then help your child.

On the Plane

Once on board, ask the flight attendant for a beverage for your child to ensure that you will have something for him to drink during takeoff to help his ears adjust to the pressure changes. Do not wait until the plane is taking off or has started the descent, as the flight attendants are busy at those times.

*Now that the restrictions on beverages has eased, you can purchase a beverage in the boarding area and be prepared.

As traveling mom Gilly noted, people tend to get friendlier two to three hours into flight, once they see what kind of parent you are.

> **People tend to react better and relax if you make eye contact, smile, and say things like, "Please let me know if he is kicking your seat or bothering you." They want to know that you will take responsibility for your child on that flight.**

I also think it doesn't hurt to bring something like a bag of chocolate kisses and pass them out to those around you. Most everyone likes chocolate—and if not, they will usually appreciate the kind gesture!

Breastfeeding

For me, breastfeeding was a wonderful asset to our travels. It was a soothing way to put my son to sleep amidst the chaos and noise of big cities and airports. If you plan on breastfeeding during your trip,

- wear a comfortable bra;

- bring a light blanket for cover;

- bring along bottles of expressed breast milk for in-flight feeding (If your baby is distraught and needs feeding, please wait until the pilot has turned off the seat belt sign. Then breastfeed your baby and return them to the safety of the car seat as quickly as possible.);

- <u>Do not breastfeed your baby during take off and landing.</u> Yes, I did breastfeed my son - before I realized how dangerous it was to have him on my lap instead of in his own seat.

> **What good is the car seat if you don't have your baby restrained in it during the most dangerous times of the flight?**

Bring some expressed milk or water along and feed your baby a bottle during take off and landing. Even if you are full-time breastfeeding (I was), babies do fine with a bottle and it gives mom some much needed breaks if someone can help you with feedings.

- remember to drink enough fluids and eat healthy snacks to ensure a good milk supply

- bring along a hand pump in case you need to express milk.

Avent Hand Breast Pump:

http://www.JetWithKidsClub.com/breastfeeding

I wished someone had educated me more about the different breast pumps when I was a new mom I assumed that the expensive, electric ones were the best and most effective. This Avent Hand Pump was far more effective for me and easier to use than any electric pump I ever owned! (Anya's review)

 ## Ascent

The acceleration on the runway and the motion of the plane climbing may scare a child who does not understand what is occurring. Realize that to them, it is like they walked down a hall into another room of the airport, since many times they are unable to see the aircraft as a whole before boarding. Explain that the airplane will drive like a car first and then will go up into the air. You know your child best. Tailor the explanation to fit your child's level of development, experience, and fears.

Your facial expressions will be a cue to your child. If you have a fear of flying, there are books and audio courses available to purchase online that address this fear and can be found when searching under the topic "fear of flying."

Books About The Fear Of Flying:

http://www.JetWithKidsClub.com/tools

Distract your child during takeoff; if he is interested in looking out of the window, point out the trees or the cars below. Remember to have him eat or drink something to assist the ears in adjusting to the changing pressure.

> **You may *not* get out of your seat during the ascent. Listen for the pilot's instruction to know when it is safe to get up from your seat.**

 ## Cruising at 37,000 Feet

1. <u>Pay attention to the flight crew</u>. Do not talk when they are speaking; be a good example to your child. The information they give you may save your life or your child's.

Jet With Kids:
Taking the Fear Out of Flying
WITH YOUR KIDS!

140

The seat belt sign is on during take-off, landing, and during turbulence. Please note however, even when the seat belt sign is turned off, you are encouraged to keep your seat belt buckled at all times while seated. The airlines realize that people will need to use the restroom and stretch their legs during flight (this can be very important in the prevention of DVTs). This does not mean that you are safe from turbulence while doing these things.

2. <u>Prevent DVTs (Deep Vein Thrombosis—blood clots that form in the deep veins of the lower extremities).</u> There are certain conditions that will increase your chances of getting a DVT (which can be fatal and can occur in young, healthy people as well as the elderly).

Conditions that increase the likelihood of DVTs:

- Immobility (sitting for a long period of time on long flights, train ride, etc.)

- Post surgery

- Medical conditions that cause the blood to clot easier than normal

- Women taking birth-control pills or hormone-replacement therapy

- Pregnancy

- Obesity

Elderly people, who are less mobile, as well as those with cancer or heart failure, are at an increased risk for DVTs, also. Consult with your physician before flying if you are at an increased risk of DVTs.

What you can do to prevent travel-related DVTs:

• Exercise your legs about once every 30 minutes in flight. When you are seated,

- press the ball of each foot hard against the floor (increases blood flow); and

- bend and straighten your legs, feet, and toes.

• Some travelers wear compression stockings.

Compression Socks:
http://www.JetWithKidsClub.com/health

> *I really noticed a difference in how good my legs felt when wearing compression socks when flying. I tend to remove my shoes in flight and put a warmer pair of socks on as well. It is great not to have swollen legs at the end of the flight. After the first time I tried the compression socks, I sent some to my mom to wear whenever she flies.*
> *(Anya's review)*

• Stay hydrated by drinking water (avoid alcohol and soda because they cause dehydration).

• Avoid sleeping pills, which increase immobility.

• Once an hour, walk up and down the aisle to stretch your legs.

• When you deplane, walk around to increase circulation in your legs. If you develop a swollen leg or any breathing difficulties, seek immediate medical care and inform them of your recent travel.

The majority of travelers do not have problems with DVTs. However, blood clots can be very serious—sometimes fatal, and can occur in even healthy, young athletes. It is important to be educated about travel related illnesses that can occur so

Jet With Kids:
Taking the Fear Out of Flying
WITH YOUR KIDS!

142

that you can seek the appropriate medical attention if necessary.

2. Don't take your child's shoes off when walking on the plane. The floor (especially the bathroom floor) is filthy. I like Robeez shoes for my son because they are comfortable and protect his feet. **http:JetWithKidsClub.com/carryon**

3. Bring new toys (never-before-seen toys), taking out one at a time as a surprise. You can find great toy suggestions on page 110 or visit: **http://www.JetWithKidsClub.com/toys**

4. A tip for the child kicking the seat in front of him (a constant thumping on their seat back will annoy even the most patient person): Bring along duplicates of some favorite photos and tape them to the upright tray table. There will be less chance of a child's feet going up where his or her favorite photos are, and this may provide a bit of distraction as well. My son loves to look at photos of relatives and friends. This also keeps him occupied for a while as we talk about the people in the pictures.

5. Acknowledge and praise good behavior; remember that the flight process can be overwhelming to an adult; children can easily experience sensory overload en route.

 **Descent**

When the flight attendants begin walking through the cabin checking seat belts in preparation for descent, have your child eat or drink something. This will assist his ears in adjusting to the changing pressure. Begin cleaning up the area around your seat in preparation for deplaning.

> **You may *not* get out of your seat during the descent. Listen for the flight crew's instructions once you arrive at the gate. Do not unbuckle your seat belt or get out of your seat until the crew announces permission to do so.**

Chapter 17

The Flight Process: Deplaning upon Arrival

I always wait until everyone else is off of the plane before attempting to get my luggage and my child off of the plane. Use this time to gather your belongings, clean up your area, undo the car seat, and take a deep breath. The line that forms never moves fast, and a child does not understand how to get up and wait.

NOTE: I do this only when I have a long enough layover. In the case of short connections, clean and pack up before descent.

 ## Pick Up Your Room!

Pick up the area around your seats when getting off the plane. Be courteous to the next person as well as to the flight crew. This also is a good example to your child, and it is good to have him participate at an age-appropriate level.

 ## Gate Checked Items

If you gate-checked your stroller, ask the airline crew where you can pick it up. Most times your stroller will arrive at the end of the jet way right outside the plane or near the door to the gate. If your stroller does not arrive, ask the gate agent to help you locate it. Do not leave the area until you have found it or have talked to an airline representative about it, since it may just take the ramp agents a bit longer to bring it up.

Jet With Kids:
Taking the Fear Out of Flying
WITH YOUR KIDS!

144

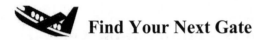 **Find Your Next Gate**

Even though the flight attendants may announce your connecting gate on the plane, please check the monitors as soon as you get off the plane. Things like gate assignments can change with a moments notice. Also, remember to locate your connecting gate as soon as possible, since it may be a lot farther away than you originally thought.

Chapter 18

The Flight Process: Baggage Claim

 Lost Luggage

If you are standing at the baggage carousel when everyone else has left and the few bags still circling are not yours, do not panic. There are a few places your luggage could be:

1. <u>One time, my luggage had been put on an earlier flight</u> (unbeknownst to me) and was waiting for me to show up! I headed toward the baggage claim office for the airline that I was flying and there it was—sitting out in a row with other bags. I didn't get an explanation from the attendant and was just happy to see my luggage safe and sound.

2. <u>Sometimes you make the connection and your luggage doesn't.</u> This also happened to me, and the funny part was that the connection was almost 2 hours long! Where my bag went during that time was a mystery.

3. <u>There is always the chance someone else took your luggage by mistake</u> (make your luggage unique!) and their luggage is still circling . . .

4. <u>You could be dealing with a lost luggage story.</u> Always verify your destination on your tags. And then realize that this does happen and usually your bag will be found and returned to you. However, it may not always be found on your timetable.

If you find yourself without your luggage, (some people get their luggage days later!) you will be glad you purchased travel insurance.

The travel insurance company many times will reimburse you up to a certain amount so that you can go out and buy things that you need. Check first with the airline on their compensation policy.

For a FREE Quote, Click on the Insure My Trip image at

http://www.JetWithKidsClub.com/links

 **Damaged Luggage**

People are human and are sometimes in a hurry. Also, there is a lot of stuff in the belly of the plane. Damage to checked luggage does happen. If it happens to you, go to the specific airline's baggage claim office, usually located by the carousel, and file a report before you leave.

Congratulations!
You are ready for family life
at 37,000 feet!

Chapter 19

Thank you to Airline Employees

First, I would like to thank all of the employees that still smile and are kind during the whole flight process. I know that their job has gotten much tougher over the years. In my years of flying, I saw firsthand the decrease in the staff-to-passenger ratio. I listened to many of them talk about how cuts were being made in benefits and perks. Like happens in many businesses, the more work for less money was starting to get to them. To top it off, the passengers were becoming more demanding and less compliant. Keep in mind what these people typically face in a workday. Many times, it is a few people who abuse a situation and ruin it for the rest. Airline employees work hard, and if they don't always smile at your little one, please don't take it personally!

Also realize something I am sure as a parent you have already acknowledged; it is usually easy to spot other people who are parents themselves! You will have a different experience interacting with all employees based on their experience with children. Many of the people that I spoke to in the travel industry are parents themselves and bring that additional knowledge to their job.

I started bringing a box of Sees chocolate candy for the flight attendants, including a short note thanking them for their smiles and hard work which made it possible for my husband and me to travel. After I had my son, I would include a note and sometimes a photo of him, thanking them for their smiles and for flying him to his grandmother's or to the beach, or wherever we were going.

Sees Candy Gifts:
http://www.JetWithKidsClub.com/gifts

Their response was amazing and unexpected. They were so bewildered that I wasn't complaining or asking them for something! This was sad to me, since I found out how very rarely they are actually thanked. I started to bring a gift of chocolate or other sweets for the gate agents as well as the pilots. They all have always been so happy that someone took the time to acknowledge their hard work. I make sure that the candy is in a sealed box and always try to buy a high-quality brand. Keep in mind that these people and their work allow you to travel!

The airline industry changes daily. It is difficult to keep up with all airlines and their ever-changing policies. You will find as you call to make reservations that if you hang up and immediately call back, you may get the exact opposite answer to the same question. This has happened to me numerous times, and I think the best defense to this is not to get upset, but to be cognizant of that fact and to be flexible.

Something that a friendly agent will gladly help you to accomplish may be something that the next agent might get upset at you for even asking. And lets face it—that is how life is. The key is to get past this and remain calm.

If you get someone who is having a bad day, do not deal with that person, if possible. Realize what I said earlier—airline employees are usually overworked and underpaid. They also deal with a stressed-out public who may not realize many other people may be calling with questions, issues, or complaints.

Having said that, I should also caution you that no matter what the first person tells you about the rules, it is up to the last person to enforce them or change them. Let's face it—the travel agent or reservation agent is not on the flight to defend why you are seated in the row behind the exit row with a car seat—the fact is you will be moving if the flight attendant decides that is what needs to be done. (This happened to my friend Diane.) Make sure that your agent checks on the current policies of the airline you will fly with and even then, go with the flow.

These people have gone through a lot of change, and they deal with a lot to test their patience daily. Many times flight attendants and pilots do back-to-back flights and end up after a long, tiring day, far away from their comfortable beds, hugs from their children, and the ability to "get away from the office" before they turn around and do it again. Home-cooked meals are not an option in hotels, and sitting around waiting for flights gets old quickly.

> **A small box of candy and a thank-you note go a long way to show your thanks. Make it genuine and offer it with a smile and no expectations.**

Many times I was given a strange look, and it was only when they realized that I wasn't trying to get anything for it, that they smiled at me. I was at a friend's party in San Francisco about 8 years ago, and a flight attendant there actually recognized me. She remembered the flight with the Sees candy! Spread some happiness and good chocolate!

 ## Flight Attendants

I wanted to write especially about flight attendants, since they are oftentimes under-appreciated and viewed as only being there to provide beverages and assistance with fitting over-sized bags into the overhead compartment.

As Renée, who had a 36-year career as a flight attendant said, "Flight attendants are there for your safety. That is our number one role." When they ask you to comply with the rules of the aircraft, please realize that their motivation is nothing more than concern for your safety and the safety of others.

Jan Brown-Lohr, a flight attendant for 25 years, states that after she survived that tragic crash in 1989, she struggled with how best to react to mothers who were holding their children.

Jet With Kids:
Taking the Fear Out of Flying
WITH YOUR KIDS!

150

I know I got in trouble one time when I tried to get a mother to move so that her lap child could sit in the seat and she took it personally. I was so focused on the safety of her child that I didn't take into account that she was one of those who was going to take it as criticism of her mothering skills because that is never where I was. I always focused on the priority, and that child was the priority. (Jan Brown-Lohr, Flight Attendant, 25 years experience)

Flight Attendants are onboard primarily for your safety.

We are on board primarily for your safety [and] your child's safety. We have quite a few medical things on the airplane. Although, we're not doctors but we are trained for a lot of emergencies. We are trained for medical emergencies, fighting fires onboard, and of course for emergency landings. We are there for your comfort as well . . . trying to find seats for your family to sit together isn't an unreasonable request. . . . If you've ordered a vegetarian meal and it didn't show up, or there's something your child won't eat, see if the flight attendant can go up to first class and get you something different. I don't think those are unreasonable [requests]. (Flight Attendant A, 28 years experience)

As flight attendant, Renée pointed out, if your child needs to use the restroom while beverages are being served, it is okay to ask the flight attendant to move the cart. That is their job, and no matter what their response, you should not ever make your child feel bad for needing to use the restroom. However, if the plane is taking off, landing, or in turbulence, you all must remain in your seat with your seat belts fastened.

In my interviews with flight attendants, numerous times they mentioned they are not there to baby-sit your children. They did state that they would be happy to watch your child if you were alone and had to use the restroom. However, I was shocked to hear that some mothers have told flight attendants that they need a break and try to hand the child over, or that they were going to sleep and could the flight attendant watch their little one. Please respect the designated role of the flight attendant.

Bottom line is this—listen to the flight attendants. They are there for your safety and have a lot of experience, and most times they have a good reason for what they expect from you. Do not argue with them, as they have the final say and you may find yourself being thrown off a flight with high penalties to pay just for arguing. If you run into a crew that seems to be treating you unfairly, record their names and flight numbers and contact the airline's customer-relations division. Remember that they are human, too, and not all of them will be as child/people-friendly as you prefer.

Chapter 20

Business Travel and Family Travel

The following article written by Joe Sharkey and published in the online version of *The New York Times* presents the view some business travelers have about flying with children. http://travel2.nytimes.com/2006/07/25/business/25road.html?adxnnl=1&fta=y&adxnnlx=1168294910-yLx7AJNWPdkEVyzzhfoFHg

I know there are a lot of different opinions about children traveling. Some of the loudest and harshest comments are from those who have experienced the negative effects of having children in their environment. Let me explain.

I mentioned that I had many times been upgraded to first class due to my frequent flier status. This was a great experience for me for many reasons. I met some fascinating people in those front rows. Some I met were owners of corporations and patents, but many also owned ulcers and hectic schedules; these people flew more than they drove.

I was amazed that many of them did not have down time to recoup from jet lag or after a long flight. Travel Agent Bob Robar reminds travelers that the airplane may be the only place for some people to sleep and get rest.

Many were expected to complete big deals or lead important meetings once they arrived at their destination. Their view of children was mixed. Many were parents themselves or had nieces and nephews, and were understanding of children traveling. However, these flights were often filled with reports to finish or notes to review before meetings. An unruly child who was screaming or kicking the seat while being ignored by his parent was an incredible distraction for these business travelers.

Travel agent Bob Robar says, *"Especially if you are booking a child in first class, be conscientious of other travelers who are paying a lot of money for those seats; kids need to be educated on how to behave in first class."*

> **I think as parents we need to realize that our children have every right to be on the airplane, however, not everyone on the flight needs to be affected by our children being there.**

Many times traveling families are on vacation, or excited about their trip. It is easy to forget that for some this is their workday and they are merely commuting, and many times need to get work completed during the flight.

Everyone who takes off on the runway is leaving the city for a different reason. Some passengers may have just lost a parent and are heading home to a funeral while others are going to see their son or daughter off to combat. Others may be heading out on their honeymoon while a newly divorced young man is miserably reliving the custody battle he is returning from.

You've got people that are scared to death, it's their first flight. It's amazing how many people are taking their first flight! There's people that are . . . going to a funeral or coming back from a funeral; there's people that are on honeymoons. . . . You've got a huge variety of reasons why these people have all come together to go somewhere. (Bob Robar, Travel Agent, 42 years experience)

If we all recognize the different reasons for travel, and take responsibility for our children and their actions, there may not be so much animosity toward children on planes. As Peter Contini, M.D., so wonderfully summarized:

People are not bothered by kids who misbehave. People are bothered by kids who misbehave and their parents don't do anything about it. So don't be afraid to discipline your child on an airplane, don't be afraid to give them a time out. There's ways to give time outs on airplanes. Don't break from your routine of discipline . . . for hopes of making a happy child. (Peter Contini, M.D., 8 years experience)

 ## Family Joining the Business Trip

For the child that is along for the business trip, it is important to role-play before you ever leave your home. Teach them (age appropriately) how to make eye contact, shake a hand and say hello. It is usually an unexpected moment when the family runs into the boss or upper management. For one parent, this unexpected meeting happened on the flight to their destination!

> **Do not be frustrated if your child does not recognize the importance of this stranger. Instead, prepare ahead of time by introducing them to others and role-playing. Teach them to make eye contact, speak politely, and smile when meeting someone.**

My 2 year old has already learned the handshake. Practice in daily life and you will be surprised at how fast children respond.

Chapter 21

In Summary

I covered a lot of things in this resource and it can seem very overwhelming to some people, especially if you are new to flying. I wrote from the heart and about things that many times I had learned the hard way. As I pointed out before, it can be challenging to fly with children – if you are unprepared and rely on others to provide what you as a family need on your journey.

As parents, we have the responsibility of doing everything possible to protect our children and keep them safe. We also have a responsibility to prepare them for life in the real world – and that includes at 37,000 feet! Congratulations on completing this resource – you are well on your way to becoming a parent "certified to fly with children"!

I have found that if you talk to your children and remember that they are experiencing this from a different perspective, you will have a better chance of a more enjoyable trip. I have always loved to fly and loved the experience of the airport. It may surprise you at how well your children adapt to changing situations if you prepare them ahead of time. Give them a fair chance – and don't be fearful of flying with them!

Jet With Kids:
Taking the Fear Out of Flying
WITH YOUR KIDS!

156

Don't be in such a rush to get to your destination that you miss experiencing this adventure with your children. In the fast-paced world of airports, the whole world comes together for moments and then jets off in different directions. Stop and observe, take a deep breath and make your journey part of your vacation!

Chapter 22

Thank you!

Thank you to the incredible people I interviewed for sharing their time and stories, their laughs, and their sorrows with me. I have enjoyed gathering this information. I also want to thank my family for being so supportive while I worked *way* more than I should have. Thank you for believing in me and encouraging me when I was hit with rejection, and always loving me! Thank you to my son, who is a great little world traveler, always adapting to change.

Thank you especially to Rachel and Cliff – this would never have been completed without your encouragement, hard work, love and support! Also a big thank you to Jane Robinson for editing, Jason Snyder, who covered the technical side of things, to Elizabeth Haase, our graphic designer and cheerleader, to "Ra" for increasing the ratio, and to the 3 ½ amigos – who are my motivation and foundation!

I thank God that I have been blessed with parents who saw the advantages of traveling and a husband who introduced me to the rest of the world. Thanks (*Khawp khun kha)*, Cliffy!

-Anya Clowers, RN, Traveling Mom

Jet With Kids:
Taking the Fear Out of Flying
WITH YOUR KIDS!

158

Chapter 23

Useful Travel Website Links

For Great Travel Website Links, Visit:

http://www.JetWithKidsClub.com/links

Chapter 24

Send in Your Travel Tip

Do you have a tip for flying with children?

**Email your tip to mytip@JetWithKids.com or visit our website
http://www.JetWithKidsClub.com
and enter your tip in our tip box on the homepage.**

This resource will be updated periodically, and your tip could be included!

View our resources along with pictures, reviews and links to all of the products mentioned in this book on our website:

**Resources:
http://www.JetWithKidsClub.com/resources**

**Products:
http://www.JetWithKidsClub.com/products**

**Product Reviews:
http://www.JetWithKidsClub.com/reviews**

Jet With Kids:
Taking the Fear Out of Flying
WITH YOUR KIDS!

160

ABOUT THE AUTHOR

Anya Clowers, a registered nurse, mother, and travel expert has enjoyed aviation travel for over 30 years. Starting as a 3-year-old toddler on her first international flight, to living on a Greek Island as a young adult, and now as a mother flying internationally with her toddler, she has always enjoyed aviation travel and the benefits of seeing the world.

Her nursing career allowed her to work alongside community nurses in Nottingham, England as well as care for the many international patients at the Mayo Clinic Hospitals. She has also held positions as a Clinical Research Nurse, working with a Stanford Hospital surgeon and a medical device company on a study that gained national media attention and was featured on CNN. Post-surgical care was her specialty at both Sutter Davis Hospital in Davis, CA and Mayo Clinic in Rochester, MN. She was the first nurse to work in Minnesota at Mayo while residing in California. This frequent travel (a 2000 mile commute to work) allowed her to become acquainted with many airline employees and gain a deeper appreciation for airline travel.

Anya Clowers has also written ***So Your Child Is Flying Alone...What You Need to Know About Flying as an Unaccompanied Minor!*** *(http://www.FlyUM.com)*

Visit this author at http://www.JetWithKidsClub.com where you can find Jet With Kids newsletters, travel products, product reviews, and more!

ORDER INFORMATION FORM

1) **Website orders:**
   www.JetWithKidsClub.com (pay with a PayPal account – credit card, bank account)

2) **Postal mail orders**:
   Send payment (check or money order payable to Jet Seven, Inc.) with this form to:

   > Jet Seven, Inc.
   > Anya Clowers, RN
   > 11230 Gold Express Drive
   > #310-402
   > Gold River, CA 95670-4484

3) **Email orders:** orders@JetWithKidsClub.com

4) **Fax orders:** 916-967-7103. Fax this form with your contact information.

Please send: (I understand that I may return the book for a full refund – for any reason, no questions asked**.)**

> Jet With Kids: Taking the Fear Out of Flying...WITH YOUR KIDS!
> By Anya Clowers, RN, Traveling Mom

> Quantity: _____ $19.95/book

Sales tax: Please add 7.75% sales tax for sales within California.
Shipping cost:
> **U.S.:** $4.00 for first book and $2.00 for each additional book.
> **International:** $9.00 for first book, $5.00 for each additional book.

*Shipping rates for international are estimate only.

Name: _____

Address: _____

City: _____ State: _____ Zip: _____

Telephone: _____

Email address: _____

*Large quantity discounts available.   **Fundraising opportunities available.

For more information, please contact:
Rachel Snyder at info@JetWithKidsClub.com or 916-853-9619.

Jet With Kids:
Taking the Fear Out of Flying
WITH YOUR KIDS!

164

ORDER INFORMATION FORM

1) **Website orders:**
www.JetWithKidsClub.com (pay with a PayPal account – credit card, bank account)

2) **Postal mail orders**:
Send payment (check or money order payable to Jet Seven, Inc.) with this form to:

> Jet Seven, Inc.
> Anya Clowers, RN
> 11230 Gold Express Drive
> #310-402
> Gold River, CA 95670-4484

3) **Email orders:** orders@JetWithKidsClub.com

4) **Fax orders:** 916-967-7103. Fax this form with your contact information.

Please send: (I understand that I may return the book for a full refund – for any reason, no questions asked**.)**

> Jet With Kids: Taking the Fear Out of Flying...WITH YOUR KIDS!
> By Anya Clowers, RN, Traveling Mom
>
> Quantity: _____ $19.95/book

Sales tax: Please add 7.75% sales tax for sales within California.
Shipping cost:
> **U.S.:** $4.00 for first book and $2.00 for each additional book.
> **International:** $9.00 for first book, $5.00 for each additional book.
*Shipping rates for international are estimate only.

> Name: _____
>
> Address: _____
>
> City: _____State: _____ Zip: _____
>
> Telephone: _____
>
> Email address: _____

*Large quantity discounts available.   **Fundraising opportunities available.

For more information, please contact:
Rachel Snyder at info@JetWithKidsClub.com or 916-853-9619.